MAKE MONEY CONSISTENTLY TRADING OPTIONS

The Basics of Stocks and ETFs Options Trading for Maximum Profits in the Markets Daily

By Dr Babajide A. Alalade

Copyright © 2018, Dr Babajide A. Alalade

ALL RIGHTS RESERVED. No part of this publication may be reproduced, stored in a retrieval system, or transmitted, in any form or by any means, electronic, mechanical, photocopying, recording, or otherwise, except as permitted under Section 107 or 108 of the 1976 United States Copyright Act, without either the prior written permission of the Publisher, or authorization through payment of the appropriate per-copy fee to Copyright Clearance Center, Inc., 222 Rosewood Drive, Danvers, MA 01923, (978)750-8400, fax (978)646-8600, or on the web at www.copyright.com. Requests to the Publisher for permission should be addressed to the Permissions Department, MarketBooks.com, tel (443)353-9886, fax (855)778-7797 or support@marketsbooks.com. Or go to: http://www.copyright.com/content/cc3/en/toolbar/productsAndSolutions/right slink/openurl_generator.html

Limit of liability/Disclaimer of Warranty: While the publisher and author have used their best efforts in preparing this book, they make no representations or warranties with respect to the accuracy or completeness of the contents of this book and specifically disclaim any implied warranties of merchandise or fitness for a particular purpose. No warranty may be created or extended by sales representatives or written sales materials. The advice and strategies contained herein may not be suitable for your situation. You should consult with a professional where appropriate> neither the publisher nor author shall be liable for any loss of profit or any other commercial damages, including but not limited to special, incidental, consequential, or other damages.

For general information on our other products and services or for technical support, please contact our Customer Care Department within the United States at support@marketsbooks.com or 443-353-9886.
HiQ Traders Markets Research, LLC publishes in a variety of print and electronic formats and by print-on-demand. Some material included with standard print versions of this book may not be included in e-book or in print-on-demand. If this book refers to media such as a CD or DVD that is not included in the version you purchased, you may download this material at marketsbooks.com. For more information about all of Babajide Alalade's books and products, visit marketsbooks.com.

This publication is designed to provide accurate and authoritative information in regard to the subject matter covered. It is sold with the understanding that the author and the publisher are not engaged in rendering legal, accounting, or other professional service.

First Published in the United States of America.
ISBN 978-1-940974-02-6; ISBN: 978-1-940974-03-3 (eBook)
Published and Distributed in the United States of America by HiQ Traders Markets Research, Delaware
Sold and Distributed by MarketsBooks.com and various online market vendors.

The Basics of Stocks and ETFs Options
Trading for Maximum Profits
in the Markets Daily

MAKE MONEY
CONSISTENTLY TRADING OPTIONS

OPTIONS TRADE SECRETS FROM A SEASONED OPTION TRADER
DR. BABAJIDE A. ALALADE

A Note to the Reader from Dr Babajide A. Alalade

The Purpose of writing this Book

I have spent years in the markets, most of my experience were in the forex and options markets. I have been so intrigued by these two because of the amount of leverage they possess, and the amazing returns you get from them. To put it this way, leverage means you could make money, in essence control an asset in the market, like a stock price or a currency pair and benefit from the profits by using a lesser amount of money compared to what you could have in relation to the amount of profit.

The successful people in history are very good at using leverage to increase their wealth. The law of Pareto [26] (the popular 80-20 rule or the law of vital few or sometimes called the principle of factor sparsity) states that for most live events, approximately 80% of the effect comes from 20% of the causes. In reality this most especially true! Now, apply this here, to get ahead in life, 80% of your success comes from 20% of your efforts. So clearly, you would need to find what these 20% of the efforts are and then concentrate on them.

Therefore, to truly make money trading you need to know how to use less to make more, and options trading and forex gives you just that consistently if you learn how to utilise them properly well.

After these years, approximately twelve, in the markets, I have discovered that history repeats itself and do so in many different ways, and I have learnt to apply this to stock trading, it means historically, stock prices repeat themselves in cycles. Therefore, knowing these patterns and learning how to anticipate them correctly at least 20% of the time could make a huge difference to your trading career.

I have discovered and designed my own trading around the chart pattern recognition techniques to enable me to capture profits consistently in the markets. Most of the most profitable traders in history learnt how to use leverage, and in trading stock markets, for you to maximise leverage you MUST learn how to trade options.

George Soros made almost more than a billion dollars from the yen carry trade early 2013 for his funds[25], similarly veteran traders like David Einhorn of Greenlight Capital, Daniel Loeb of Third Point LLC and Kyle Bass's Hayman Capital Management LP, also made HUGE trading profits by trading the Japanese yen[25]. The yen lost nearly 20 percent of its value against the dollar between November 2012 and early February 2013 due to the pressure from the new Japanese government on the Bank of Japan to ease monetary policy more aggressively in order to control and hence reduce deflation[25].

John Arnold, a hedge fund manager and former Enron star trader who is currently worth $3.5 billion, retired at the age of 38. He made his fortune through Centaurus Advisors, his own energy trading firm[6]. He recently closed his fund group and returned all cash to investors and now free to pursue other interests[15]. He was known as the 'king of gas' at some point, making some real cash from gas contracts.

All these people above learnt the power of leverage in the markets and used them to their ultimate advantage. The purpose of this book in your hands is to give you the inside know-how to do the same consistently.

I would go through some historical charts periodically in this book and show how to search for them. I would also give a list of stocks on my watch-list ready to bounce, and I could send them to you regularly during open live market sessions for you to see what I trade and do the same at your will. These could make you outstanding gains beyond your imaginations.

I have ensured that this book is simple and readable for all, whether you are a *newbie or a pro*. This would give you the opportunity to learn from the experts and stand tall on the shoulders of giants.

Here in this book, in your hands, I would take you through the world of options like you have never been before.

This is to show you how to spot the stocks and specifically options with higher probabilities of profits. I would discuss the rudimentary basics of stock, index and ETFs options, the Greeks, using the power of using Spreads and Combinations, and how to use beta options strategies to make profits from the markets.

My aim and desire is that by the time you put this book down you would get more that value of the money you spent purchasing it, and that it would be truly a blessing to you, your family and your friends. This is my ultimate joy and when that is done, I would know that I have succeeded. Drop me an email (support@marketsbooks.com) to share your success stories. I would endeavour to include your comments in subsequent editions of this book.

Thank You.

For your Maximum and Consistent Profits,

Dr Babajide A. Alalade,
Ellicott City, MD

Acknowledgements

This book is a dream come true, once again! We stand on the shoulder of giants this enables us to see far and wide in to horizon, and the farther you can see, so is how further your vision would go. Without the support of certain people in my life this endeavour would not be a reality, if I failed to mention your name(s) I certainly do appreciate you, I did not intend to forget, Thank You, I am forever grateful!

My special thanks goes to all. to my wonderful teachers who have helped and supported me along the way: Mark Anastasi, Robert G. Allen, Simon Coulson, Rhonda Byrne, Anthony Robbins, Robert Kiyosaki, Scott Fox, and Wallace D. Wattles.

I would love to thank Gabrielle, Arielle & Daniel; Dr (Late) John & Mrs Julie Alalade (my parents); Dr T.O. Alalade, Oxford, UK; Dr T. Alalade, Dr O. Taiwo, Dr Aderemi Alalade, Wales, UK; Bola Alalade; Dr Jimmy Agbaosi MD, Memphis, TN; Mr B.R. Fujah, Esq., BRAF Logistics, London; Mr Femi Ojo, Essex, UK; Bosede Ireti-Ogo Deborah Olanrewaju, Lekki, Lagos, Nigeria.

My eternal gratitude goes to Dr Dib Datta, Dr Wunmi Ogunnoiki, Dr Prabas Misra, Dr Vincent I. Bamgboye, Dr

Shahnaz Nawaz, Dr Lorraine Johnston, Dr Barry Marshall, Dr Mumtaz Rashid; these are forever my angels. Thank You!

To all those who think I am a failure, thank you, I wouldn't have pushed myself this far, I wanted to proof to myself that everyone has a seed in them for greatness, without your negatives there would not have been such a positive force from me.

Thanks to the entire members of the StockCharts.com and OptionsXpress.com team for the excellent charts used in these materials, you guys do a truly amazing job, keep it up!

You'll always miss 100% of the shots you don't take.
— Wayne Gretzky, Hockey Player

A smooth sea never made a skilful mariner.
— *English proverb*

Contents

A Note to the Reader from Dr Babajide A. Alalade — 5

Acknowledgements — 9

Introduction — 17

Chapter One: Options Basics — 23

Chapter Two: Basic Options Strategies — 45

Chapter Three: Trading Options: Getting Started in Options Trading — 65

Chapter Four: Options Greeks — 85

Chapter Five: Effect of Dividends on Option Pricing — 95

Chapter Six: Advantages of Options Trading — 111

Chapter Seven: ETFs Options — 121

Chapter Eight: Leverage ETFs and Options: How to trade them — 139

Chapter Nine: ETFs vs. Index Options — 147

Chapter Ten: Beta Options Strategies — 159

Conclusion — 217

List of Options Exchanges in the United States — 219

List of ETFs creators	221
About the Author	223
Further Reading	227
Disclaimer	229
Bibliography	233

Introduction

If you have ever wondered about knowing the simple and proven techniques of making money consistently daily and weekly trading the equity (stock) options in the United States markets then this is Home!

The secrets I am about to reveal to you in this book about the options market is so powerful that I can guarantee that they would change your live forever. If anything, in fact this book should considered illegal by the so-called elite traders in Chicago and New York.

In this book, I would take you through the basics of stock options, the Greeks, the power of using Spreads and Combinations, the effects of dividends on Options Pricing, compare stock options, Index Options and the ETFs Options. I would expose to you the power of using leveraged ETFs Options, and our proprietary Beta Options Strategies used at hiqtraders.com, to generate outstanding gains consistently from the markets.

I am about to show you how to make outstanding gains in the stock market like never before, this is the same secret used by the 7-digit Chicago Board of Trade traders (CBOE), in this book you have them at your fingertips. This is the map to outstanding gains in the stock market you have been searching for. The information in this book is worth over $250,000 alone! Today, it is yours for a token. In the market, knowledge is not Power, it is the use of it that is! When a fool and his money meets a wise man, by the time they spend some few hours together there would exchange ideas, and this includes what they brought to the table. The fool leaves with the wisdom and the wise man leaves with the money. Sad as it seems, if it happens only once then it for the better for the fool, then he would not repeat the same mistakes. He would be wiser.

Now the purpose of my writing of this piece is to save you heart-aches if you desire to invest or trade the markets, especially the stock and ETFs options markets to make money. My mission is to save you lots of heart aches, and make you one of the elite traders in the world. By the power of simple association, through the reading of this book, you would be tapping in to the deep fountain of knowledge that I have come to possess by over seven years of studying what makes money in the markets, especially in the United States.

If you intend to spend $15,000 of your life-savings for example in investments, would it not make common sense for you to find an expert in the endeavour you are about to pursue. In fact, only professional hire experts anyway. Look around, if anyone intends to advance in their chosen career they usually have mentors or someone that literarily takes them by the hands.

I am sure that you have tried various trading systems before, and you have burnt money, if this is your story, Welcome! It was once my story till I met someone that transformed by life, within five weeks of trading I was debt-free my life was transformed, totally. True, this might not be your goal, but you can do whatever you want with the cash you made.

Look at the chart below on **ULTA (ULTA: NASDAQ)** for example:

This stock was spotted on September 12, 2013 by our analysts and we bought calls on the stocks, and sold the next day. See the next chart, this is what happened to the price of the stock......on September 13, 2013:

ULTA closed the day before at about $100 per share, and the next day opened to above $117!!! Now imagine what happened to calls we bought! We made over 650% gain in less than 24 hours! FYI: this chats were live chats which we saved from our paid subscription to Stockcharts.com, so we could not have manipulated it, and more so we made our marking on the indicators to indicate our pressure points before we entered the market to purchase the calls. The first was the end-of-day chart for Sept 12 (see top left of the chart) and the other was Sept 13.

If this is what you are looking for then you have it in your hands. This book is written for the beginner and the expert, so if you want to, you could skip chapters to where you find comfortable. Now, for options you need to right about so many things: the price, the anticipated price move and time of the price move for the stock, and also purchase the right options in terms of the price and expiration month as well. So clearly, options is an arena for the experts, but we are here to demystify it totally!

In this book these sort of trades we shall uncover, showing you the straight path to amazing riches in trading the U.S. equity markets.

Over the decade option trading volume has increased and so also is the opportunity that has been created for everyone, the level playing is truly level, yes it is flat. Trust me it is called 'level-playing' field for a reason. Oh yeah!

I would not bore you with all the academic stuff in most options books, we shall go right to the real meat.

Get Started!!!

Go online to ***www.hiqtraders.com***, 24 hours a day, 7 days a week, register and be on your way to Huge Returns Trading Options

December, 2013

Dr Babajide Alalade,
Ellicott City, MD

Chapter One:
Options Basics

In this chapter I am going to describe what options mean, their use and the advantage they possess. Typically, options gives you options literarily. They are derivative instruments, that is, they possess their power essentially by being referenced to an underlying financial asset. Now, I guess that if you are new to trading these first few lines would probably put you off, but trust me, I would endeavour you to just stick out here with me, continue reading and you would eventually make sense of everything.

By definition a stock option is contract between two parties that gives the holder (purchaser) of the right to, but not the obligation, to buy or sell shares of the underlying financial instrument at a specific agreed price (i.e. strike price) on or before, not after, a given date.

Now, mind the words, *underlying financial instrument*, which means this could be forex, stocks, Exchange traded funds (ETFs), currency ETFs, commodities and futures, bonds and interest rates. They could also be traded on common indexes like the AMEX, CBOE, NYSE, PHLX, PSE), on U.S. Treasury securities, and on foreign currencies on floor of the Philadelphia Stock Exchange, Inc. (PHLX). For the purposes of this discussion we would restrict ourselves to stock and ETFs options in this book for most part.

The second part, *specific agreed price (strike price)*, at this price the seller of the option contract must either buy the underlying instrument from the holder of the contract or sell the underlying instrument to the holder of the option contract.

Thirdly, at a 'specific agreed price on or before, not after, *a given date*' – which means that after this specific given date (i.e. expiration date), the option ceases to exist. On or before this date the seller of the options contract must buy or sell the underlying shares from or to the holder of the contract at the specified agreed price at the exchange of the contract prior, *upon the request of the buyer*.

Options could be call options, put options or combination of both. As a trader you would buy a call option if you anticipated the share price to rise higher or a put option if you expect the price to fall. As an option seller, if you thought they price of a share would fall you would sell call options, and you would sell puts if you expected the price to rise.

You could use a combination of the calls and puts options to achieve different trading objectives depending on the direction or 'non-direction of the market'. Options are very useful and robust in that they are very flexibility and they add flavour to stock and ETFs trading. Without options you either buy shares expecting them to rise or you sell them by depositing some money to cover the price as a margin with your broker that is if you have so much money anyway. The added advantage about options trading is that you do not have to be bullish or bearish, with options you can decide or stay undecided in the markets.

Options offer some of the following benefits;

- It protects your stock holdings from a decline in market price
- It literally gives you the opportunity to make money on your shares if they do not move up or down, effectively collecting 'rent' on your shares
- It gives the leverage to benefit from a stock rise or drop in value without actually intending to buying the stock
- Enables traders to correctly position themselves in the market to profit from an impending stock price move even if they do not know or want to guess the direction of the move
- Collect dividends on the shares without owning the stock at all
- Gives traders the opportunity to buy the stock back at much lower price

Stock options are regulated by the Securities and Exchange Commission (SEC), and they are traded on the floor of the following U.S. exchanges: The Chicago Board Options Exchange, Inc. (CBOE), the New York Stock Exchange, Inc. (NYSE), the Pacific Stock Exchange, Inc. (PSE), the American Stock Exchange, Inc. (AMEX), and the Philadelphia Stock Exchange, Inc. (PHLX).

When you enter any order an order to buy or sell option contract(s) it could be filled at any of the exchanges for the best available price. You don't really need to care about where your order was filled, sometimes your broker tell you, but it does not really matter, a filled order is a filled order, period.

Remember, that I said earlier that options is a contract between two parties at least, and one the parties is obliged to deliver the underlying financial instrument at a specific price on a specific date, so therefore this agreement must be enforced, right. This is where the Options Clearing Corporation (OCC) comes in.

The Options Clearing Corporation guarantees and clears the transactions of all option contracts listed the on the U.S. securities exchanges to ensure that the rights and all other obligations as stipulated within option contracts are fulfilled. These U.S. exchanges includes the AMEX, CBOE, NYSE, PSE, and the PHLX. Liquidity cannot always be guaranteed in the markets under some extreme conditions making it difficult to obtain an ideal price to fill for your contracts.

Despite its relatively new existence options has quickly gained prominence in the financial industry. In fact, exchange-traded options since they have been listed and regulated in 1973 have become a great indispensable tool in maintaining and encouraging liquidity and most especially participation in the financial markets today. Exchange-traded options offers an orderly, efficient, flexible tool with immense leverage and limited risk today.

The Beauty of Equity options

In most cases, except very few exceptions, all equity stock option contracts are bundled and sold as contacts, and each represent 100 shares. That is, when you hold 1 option contract you essentially control 100 shares of the particular company's stock or underlying financial instrument. As discussed above, the strike price of a stock option is the specified share price at which the stock could be purchased or sold by the holder of the option contract(s) at any point in time that the holder of the option contract decides to exercise their option, prior to the expiration of the option contract.

In most cases strike prices are listed in increments of 2.5, 5, or 10 points, depending on the current market value of the underlying stocks (or financial instrument).

The market prices of options contracts are determined by the market forces of buyers and sellers on the exchanges, and they are set by a complex Black-Scholes formula, see more detailed options book for the formula for extensive mind-boggling calculations or formulas on Black-Scholes models, but in all sincerity it is more or less a waste of time to learn the formula, you just need to make profits, and that is what I am here to show you.

Options vs. Common Stocks

I already explained that options are derivatives, that is, they derive their price value with respect to the respective company's stock price or the financial instrument's quoted price. So clearly options cannot exist on their own. I also described that here are two types of options, calls and puts. When you purchase a put option as the buyer you are anticipating that the price of the underlying stock would fall, and as the price of the underlying stock falls the value of the put options increases. In a similar manner, if you purchase call options on a stock your expectation is that the value of the underlying stock would rise, so as the price of the underlying stock rises, the value of the call options rises as well. What I described just now is buying naked calls and puts options. As you buy and hold these options, calls or puts, the seller on the other hand has the opposite expectations compared to the buyer of the put and call options.

The seller of the call options expects the underlying stock to fall or to remain stagnant so that the cost of selling the options to take profit or exercising them by the holder (plus commission costs) would deter the holder from exercising the options or reduce the risk of seller for being assigned. Similarly, the seller of the put options expects the underlying stock to rise or at least remain stagnant so that the cost of selling exercising them by the holder (plus commission costs) would deter the holder from exercising the options or reduce the risk of seller for being assigned.

Options and equity stocks are both listed on the exchanges, the exchange where the equities and or their respective options are listed varies, but it is not essential to go it to that in this book. It is a waste of time. You place your order to buy or sell options via your broker just like the way you place buy and sell orders for stocks with your broker.

Much like stocks, options price can be tracked and the volume watched, but surprisingly I have found that sometimes with very light volume on an option the price could jump or fall without any degree of proportionality to the moves seen in the price of the underlying asset or financial instrument, this is where you need to learn options greeks in a later chapter.

Options are in much the same way as common stocks, on the floor of the exchanges listed above in this chapter, but there are has been a steady and consistent move in to online trading for the options like most financial instruments these days. However, some contracts are still traded via the old open-cry mechanisms.

As I described before in options, each options contract gives you the right but not the obligation to buy or sell 100 shares (per option contract) of the underlying stock or financial instrument at a specified or given price per share for a given period of time, that is before the expiration of the option contract.

Some of the *differences* between options and stocks are that in contrast to the commonly traded stocks, options expire. They decay with time, as they approach their expiration dates their value goes down rapidly, but not in all cases, here in this book we would show you how to find those exceptional ones. Unlike the commonly traded stocks whereby if you bought them and the value goes down you could hold them in long enough till the prices recover, options are not designed that way. They expire therefore you have to be right on the price move of the underlying asset prior to the expiration. Sometimes the price of the underlying goes the way you want and the option only moves a little, your luck. If the option contract you hold is not or exercised prior to its expiration date, it ceases to exist as a financial instrument.

Options are constantly created by the exchange depending on the number of buyers and sellers showing interest. There is no fixed number of options on a particular financial instrument this is unlike common stocks. As an option is simply a contract between a buyer and seller as to the agreed price a buyer willing to pay to the seller to obtain this rights and that a seller is willing to grant these rights. *This is the price of the option contract.* The open interest on a particular option contract is the number of outstanding options which depends on the number of buyers and sellers interested in exchanging these rights between each other.

Unlike stocks which gives the owner part ownership of a particular company, including certain voting rights and rights to dividends if at all from time to time, options gives the holder only the opportunity to profit from the potential movement in the price of an underlying instrument, for example stocks. Following the purchase of a stock in most cases certificates are issued to your broker or sometimes to you depending on the exchange's terms and conditions, however, options are just certificates-less. The positions you hold or held on them are just printed on printed statements sent or provided online by your brokers. So options in reality are *green*!

Types of Options

Like I said earlier, there are two types of options, *calls and puts*. A call option gives its holder the right to buy an underlying security, whereas a put option conveys the right to sell an underlying security, at a specific price. To possess these rights you pay a cost, that is, *the premium*. If you buy naked calls and naked puts, the premium paid is the maximum you can lose should in case the move of the stocks either for calls or puts does not move in your favour. However, if it does, the gains from naked calls and naked puts is limitless.

For the purposes of the discussion in this book, we would be discussing the typical American-style options contracts. For example, if a stock options is quoted as say, OII Nov. 13: 90 Calls; and 1 option contract was purchased, what this means is that the purchaser or holder of the options contract (having paid the premium) has the right to purchase 100 shares of OII at $90 per share at any date prior to the expiration of the option which is the 3rd Saturday of November 2013.

Underlying Security

In the above example the underlying security is OII (Oceaneering), therefore options are also called derivatives, as they derive their value with respect to the underlying security. Each one option contract represents the right to buy or sell 100 shares of the underlying financial security (ETFs or stocks).

Strike Price

The strike price, or exercise price, of an option is the pre-agreed price at which the share of a stock can be purchased (in case of a call) or sold (in the case of a put) at any point in time at which the holder of the call or put decides to exercise his or her right as agreed at exchange of the options contract (i.e. when the options contract was purchase/sold to open the trade).

Depending on the current market price of the option strike prices are set, and they are usually close to the current share price of the underlying stock or security. Whenever the share price rises (in the case of calls) or falls (in the case of puts) more options contracts are created for these respective strike prices.

In most cases strikes prices are set at the following intervals; for stock with price at $25 or less the interval of the option strike price are $2.5; strike prices of $5-points interval for stock prices between $25 and $200; and $10 for those over is $200, but with the introduction of weekly options this may not always be the rule.

Whenever the strike price of the call option is less than the current market price of the underlying stock then it is *in-the-money* because the holder or the buyer of this call option has the right to buy the stock at a price which is less than the current market price he would paid for the same stocks if the trader went into the market at that point in time to buy it.

Similarly, the put option is said to be in-*the-money* if the strike price of the options is greater in value than the current market price of the stock, because the holder or the buyer of this put option has the right to sell the stock at a price which is greater than the current market price he would get paid for the same stocks if the trader went into the market at that point in time to sell this same shares. *At the-money options* are said to have strike price that are equal to the current market price of the stock. *Out-the-money options* are options with call strike prices that are higher than the current market price; and for puts options, *out-the-money options* are said to have strike price that are lower than the current market price of the stock.

Premium

This is the cost paid by the option buyer to obtain the right to buy or sell the underlying security, it is paid to option writer, that is, the seller of call or the seller of the put. On receipt of this payment the writer of the option (call or put) is obliged to deliver the x quantity of the shares (depending on the amount of option contracts exchanged) to the option buyer if the call is exercised. Similarly, the writer of a put option has an obligation to take delivery of the shares from an option buyer if the put is exercised.

The benefit to the writer of the option is that he or she gets to keep the premium whether the option contracts are exercised or not. For example, if I wanted to buy May 2013 QCOR 100 call options, it would be quoted as $0.5 per option contract, therefore if I wanted to buy 10 option contracts it would be ($0.5 x 1,000 shares). The premium, which is $0.5

would represent a premium payment of $50.00 per option contract ($0.5 x 100 shares). Premiums are quoted on a per share basis.

American, European and Capped Styles

In regards to the way options are exercised there are three types; American, European and the Capped. With the American-styled options, the holder of an option has the right to exercise his option at any time before the expiration date of the option (or they could simply allow the option contract to expire if they are worthless). Remember that most options (about 80%) bought expire worthless. Most of the common trade options are on the U.S stock exchanges and are automatically American styled option contracts.

For the European-styled options, they can only be exercised on expiration. Capped options can be exercised on expiration, except the option value prior to expiration reaches a pre-set value (the cap), in such a case the option gets exercised.

Closing Option Contracts

To close an option contract the buyer or the seller needs to make an opposite transaction. For example, if I bought a call option to open a trade, to close that particular trade I would need to sell the same call option of the same stock, at the same strike price and at the same expiration.

If you sold a call option to open a trade, you simply need to buy the same call option contract to close the trade, the same applies to puts. If I bought a put option to open, I would need to sell the same put at the same strike price for the same stock at the same expiration to close the trade. The opposite goes for selling a put to open a trade, you would need to buy it to close the trade.

The Option Contract

Every option contract has the following details; the underlying security, expiration date, strike price, calls/puts and price of the option. If you look at the sample option contract below: **XYZ DECEMBER 17, 2011 70 CALL AT $3.10**

Underlying security	***XYZ***
Expiration date	***DECEMBER 17, 2011***
	(i.e. Expiration month, day, year)
Strike price	***70***
Calls/puts	***CALL***
Price of the option	***$3.10***

If you sold options (calls/puts) you are short, and if you bought options contracts you are long.

XYZ DECEMBER 17, 2011 70 CALL AT $3.10

The Expiration Process

The expiration date of an option is the last day an option ceases to trade. For example, if I look at an option quoted as QCOR Nov 13: 80 Call; it means the option expires in November 2013, with a strike price of $80 and it is a call option. Therefore, since it expires November 2013, then it means it expires on the third Saturday of November 2013.

All stocks and ETFs options expire on the third Saturday following the third Friday of the expiration month. However, since all trading pits are closed on Saturdays, the last day of options trading is the third Friday. Once an option expires an options contract becomes invalid and the right to exercise it no longer exists. On expiration the brokers submit their intent to exercise their options (that is, on the request of their clients, etc.) via the OCC. More options contracts are created for the next month as soon as so forth.

Once the holder of the option decides to exercise their call or put option, they notify their broker before cut-off time for accepting exercise instructions on that day. Most brokers firms have the same cut-off times, but it would be well within your rights to enquire from your broker their cut-off time before you start trading options. Some even have different cut-off times for different classes of options.

Once the OCC receives the notice to exercise an option contract, it assigns it to their Clearing members with positions that are short the same options series. This is done fairly according to the OCC rules. See the OCC rules here below:

(http://www.optionsclearing.com/components/docs/legal/rules_and_bylaws/occ_rules.pdf).

Once the respective clearing member receives this request they would assign it to any of their clients, according to their protocols either randomly or on a first in first out basis, who hold short positions in that series. Basically the OCC stands in the middle to ensure each party meet their obligations.

Most options usually start trading at least about six to eight months before its expiration date. I would advised any one, most especially individual traders not to trader monthly options contracts till they are about one month to expiration, except for the LEAPS. The reason is that by that time most options would have established a reasonable price pattern.

Leaps® / Long-Term Options

Another innovation in options trading over the last decade or so, is the advent of Long-term Equity Anticipation Securities® (LEAPS®) or call them long-term stock options. Like all options they provide the holder the right to purchase or sell the shares of a stock at a specified price on or before a given date, but the beauty here is the date. For LEAPS it is up to three years in to future. They are like the normal everyday options asset giving all the aforementioned advantages of an option, the only difference is their date of expiration.

They are available as calls and puts, traded in the American-style. Typically the offer investor a longer term view of the price movement of a stock. If for example I saw Apple (AAPL) when it was still traded as a $50 stock, and I bought the LEAP calls options on it to sell it in three years) to sell it in three years, by buying a $250 call. It gives me the power to benefit from the price movement of an innovative company without taking the risk of losing all my funds should in case the stock collapses in value. Also since it is longer term approach, the trader does not need to worry too much about daily price fluctuations or be glued to the trading screen all day long. Similarly, the LEAPS® puts provides a hedge for substantial declines in their stocks. You could also structure spreads on LEAPS® as well. LEAPS® also have the same expiration as the normal everyday options, that is, the Saturday following the third Friday of the expiration month and all equity LEAPS® expire in January. LEAPS® also available on ADRs.

How is the Price of an Option Contract Determined?

The price of an option is determined based on the values of some important factors which would be discussed in this section. These indirectly determines the price of an option premium. These factors includes the price of the underlying shares, duration of time available until the option contract expires, interest rates, availability of cash dividends on the shares, and ultimately the volatility of the underlying share price.

Underlying Stock Price

One of the most important determinants of the price of an option is the price of its underlying stock. For example, if a call option's strike price is $35 and the underlying

Stock is trading at $40, the therefore has an intrinsic value of $ 5, the buyer of the holder of this option could exercise it buying the stock shares for $35. This option is in the money as the share price is higher that the strike price therefore it has intrinsic value, as described above. Options with intrinsic values are priced higher than those that does not have such values. Though at-the-money or out-of-the-money options do not have intrinsic value, they are not always cheap.

Option Premium = Intrinsic Value + Time Value

Now as described before there are other important factors that determine the price of an option, that is option premium, apart from the intrinsic value. I mentioned previously they are the duration of time available until expiration, availability of cash dividends on the shares, volatility of the underlying share price and the interest rates.

They all make up the remaining factor that determines the price of an option premium, the time value. Time value has a real value for in-the-money options, however for out-of-the money and the at-the-money options in most cases it is zero and in these cases the time value is equal to the option premium.

Duration of time available until expiration

As we are now aware that options are decaying assets, the further away the date that an option is due to expire the higher its price, as there is still the higher chance or probability that it may change in value prior to its expiration, and be in-the-money. As an option contract enter its expiration week, it falls rapidly in value. Sometimes this could be the opportunity to purchase options cheap enough in anticipation of an earnings release.

Other factors that could affect the price of the underlying security and would in turn affect the price of the option contract are;

1. *Availability of cash dividends on the shares*

I would explore more of this in other subsequent chapters in this book. Clearly, the issue of cash dividends on a stock usually in most cases affects the premium on the option.

As I would discuss later, the stock price usually falls by the value of the dividend paid out on the stock. If the premiums paid out on a stock is high it usually leads to a fall in the value of the call premium and in most cases cause the value of the put premium to rise. I also discussed the effects of *stock splits* on option values as well in later chapters. It usually cause a rise in the value of the growth high beta stocks.

2. *Volatility of the underlying share price.*

Volatility is the juice of any market. The ability of an underlying security whether stocks, ETFs or forex to change in value either up or down in response to any news release, economic index or even other industry related factors/news is what traders like, and it creates massive profits. So, the more volatile a stock or underlying security is, the more the premium on it.

3. *Interest Rates*

Higher interest rate usually have a positive effect on the cost of premiums especially the calls. Interest rates have a directly proportional effect on the price of call premiums, and an indirectly proportional effect on the price of put premiums.

Call and Put Prices

I have inserted below a snapshot of the option chain of Expedia (EXPE) expiring Dec 2013. In the middle of the chart you would see the current price of the EXPE stock, i.e. $63.69. Below this current price, you see different prices, for example; 40, 41, 42, etc. these are the strikes prices.

To the right and left of each strike price you would see similar columns, labelled: *last, chg, bid, ask, vol, opint and action.*

Last	Chg	Bid	Ask	Vol	Opint	Action	Strike	Last	Chg	Bid	Ask	Vol	Opint	Action
							EXPE @ 63.69							
0	0	22.50	24.30	00	0	Trade | Detail	40.00	0.05	0	0	0.05	00	33	Trade | Detail
0	0	21.50	23.30	00	0	Trade | Detail	41.00	0.05	0	0	0.05	00	363	Trade | Detail
0	0	20.96	22.90	00	0	Trade | Detail	42.00	0.03	0	0	0.05	00	118	Trade | Detail
0	0	19.80	20.30	00	0	Trade | Detail	43.00	0.02	0	0	0.05	00	101	Trade | Detail
18.00	0	18.30	20.40	00	0	Trade | Detail	44.00	0.03	0	0	0.05	00	688	Trade | Detail
15.40	0	16.80	20.00	00	0	Trade | Detail	45.00	0.02	0	0	0.05	00	204	Trade | Detail
13.46	0	15.80	18.90	00	0	Trade | Detail	46.00	0.05	0	0	0.05	00	102	Trade | Detail
5.00	0	14.80	17.60	00	0	Trade | Detail	47.00	0.12	0	0	0.05	00	1,313	Trade | Detail
13.36	0	14.20	15.90	00	2	Trade | Detail	48.00	0.10	0	0	0.05	00	1,128	Trade | Detail
12.50	0	14.50	14.80	00	2	Trade | Detail	49.00	0.10	0	0	0.05	00	838	Trade | Detail
11.47	0	13.60	13.80	00	57	Trade | Detail	50.00	0.02	0	0	0.05	00	9,179	Trade | Detail
9.10	0	8.60	8.80	00	6,249	Trade | Detail	55.00	0.05	1	0	0.10	00	9,699	Trade | Detail
4.18	0	4.10	4.40	00	7,585	Trade | Detail	60.00	0.60	0	0.50	3.60	00	4,239	Trade | Detail
1.25	0	1.20	1.25	00	2,238	Trade | Detail	65.00	2.60	0	2.50	2.60	00	466	Trade | Detail
0.15	0	0.15	0.20	00	142	Trade | Detail	70.00	6.70	0	6.40	6.80	00	117	Trade | Detail
0.05	0	0	0.05	00	237	Trade | Detail	75.00	0	0	10.70	11.50	00	0	Trade | Detail
0	0	0	0.05	00	0	Trade | Detail	80.00	17.80	0	15.20	16.40	00	0	Trade | Detail
	Jan14 Calls			(48 days to expiration)			EXPE @ 63.69							Jan14 Puts
	Apr14 Calls			(139 days to expiration)			EXPE @ 63.69							Apr14 Puts
	Jul14 Calls			(230 days to expiration)			EXPE @ 63.69							Jul14 Puts

© OptionsXpress.com. 2013

You would see some rows on the calls side (i.e. to the right) colored yellow and the same on the puts side (i.e. left). What this means is that for the calls on the right, all the options contract shaded in yellow are in-the-money, and for the puts the one shaded in yellow are in-the-money.

You would notice that for the calls options shaded in yellow their strike prices are *at or below* the current price of the underlying asset. For the puts, you would notice that for the options shaded in yellow their strike prices are *at or above* the current price of the underlying asset.

So therefore as the strike prices of the call options fall compared to the current price of the underlying asset, the premium tends to be costlier, as they are in –the-money. For the puts as the strike price of the option contracts rises compared to the current underlying asset price, the premium tends to be costlier, as they are in –the-money.

Last is the most recent traded price of the particular option contract, chg is the change compared to the day before, bid is current price you can sell your option contract, ask is the price that you would purchase your option contract, vol is the current volume of the option contract traded, opint is the open interest on that particular option contract and action is there for you to click to decide whether you want to trade (buy or sell) that particular contract.

Chapter Two:
Basic Options Strategies

One of the favourite features about options is that they can be used to produce variety of trading strategies to produce profits from the trading. You could buy or sell a call or a put, you could buy both together to open a trade, and buy a call and sell a put as a combination, and so on and so forth, depending on your overall investment or trading objectives and market outlook.

In this chapter I would outline various examples, naked calls and put, spreads and straddles and other combinations. I would not add the cost of transactions including, commission and transaction fees and tax considerations as these vary depending on your brokerages.

For the purposes of illustration in this book, I would assume that all the options discussed are American-style. What this means is that they can be exercised at any time prior to expiration.

Buying Calls

As I described earlier in the previous chapter buying a call option contract gives the buyer of the contract (who becomes the holder of the contract) the obligation or the right to buy a specified number of shares of the underlying financial instrument (stock, or ETFs shares) at the given strike price on or before the expiration date of the contract. The expiration day for U.S. style options contract is the third Saturday of the month, but apparently the last trading before that Saturday is the Friday before, so technically this options expire on the third Friday. If Friday is a holiday, the last trading day will be the day before, Thursday. Brokerage firms, however, do set earlier deadlines to notify sellers of options contracts the buyer's intention to exercise.

Reasons why we buy options contracts:

1. Calls options are bought in order to make profits from an expected rise in the underlying financial security, for example share price. As I discussed in the earlier chapter, each option contract gives the holder the right to purchase 100 shares of the underlying financial security at the specified prices.
Therefore, if I bought 1 contract of **QCOR Oct 13: 95 Calls**, it gives me the right to purchase 100 shares of QCOR common stock at a cost of $95 per share at any time before the option expires in October 2013. The

icing on the cake comes when that stock goes up in price, say $97, then that right to buy it at a fixed price of $95 becomes valuable.

If for example, you paid $1.40 per contract (actual price for each contract on October 2, 2013) and you sell at $3.0 on October 17, 2013 as the prices moves to $96.5, you could either do one of these; since your option in now in-the-money you could exercise your option and buy the shares of QCOR for $9,640* ($95 + $1.4 per options contract) and sell the shares $9,700, therefore our profit was $(9,700- 9,640) = $60 (a 2.10% profit, not even accounting for the $1.4 paid).

*(We bought 1 contract, which gives us the right to buy 100 shares).

We could also, sell you contract for $300 and remove the initial $140 paid for the contract, leaving you with a net profit of $160, this is clearly 53.33% profit. Therefore, any reasonable trader would go with this second option.

If however, the stock fell below $95 your contract could expire worthless, or worth less than you paid, I have had to sell some of my options in the past for less than it was when they were initially purchased just to savage whatever that was left. As the expiration fast approaches the value of an option contract decreases rapidly. If a trader had bought the shares of QCOR shares itself at $95 and it fell to $92, compare the loss to the value of the option contract falling from $1.4 to $0.75 (this happened at some point during this particular trade); the value of the loss in trading the shares outrightly is incomparable to trading the options.

2. You could buy calls in stock to ensure you get a favourable price. This is the same idea for buying forex calls on a particular currency which is very common among multinational companies doing deals in different currencies, doing business and mergers and acquisition across currencies or airlines to guarantee the cost of fuel and guarantee airline fares, and so on an so forth.

This is idea could be used in stocks as well. You could buy options on particular shares to be able to purchase the stock at a price in case it rises. For example, a trader want to buy the 5,000 shares of Tesla (TSLA: NASDAQ) which was trading at $62 around May 2013 and he or she does not have the funds to purchase all the shares he or she wanted, and apparently does not want to miss this opportunity. So the trader buys 1000 shares in cash, and decides to buy the remaining via options contracts, and that means the trader would buy 40 contracts of the TSLA. So if the trader bought the option say at a strike price of $62.5 to expire in about 4 months away for $2.5 per contract. Now the price of TSLA has gone up to about $160 within that period. So that was a good deal. The trader would definitely exercise the option to buy the shares of TSLA at $62.5, and may keep the shares or resell it or can just exercise the option without taking delivery of the shares itself.

So in essence the trader locks in the purchase price of the shares for the future. However, if the value declines in price, then he could simply allow the option to expire and keep the 1,000 shares. Hence the trader protected their funds and preserves their opportunity to participate in any future stock price move as well.

3. Buying calls to hedge short stock sales. Investors who for some reasons have sold shares in a stock short, in order to protect themselves go back in to the market to purchase calls on those short sales to ensure that if the price of the shares rises they can exercise and reduce their losses. Some the reasons could be that the investor has for example 4,000 shares of TSLA and the trader thinks that the shares of TSLA would decline. If the trader sold 25 call option contracts and use some of the proceeds to buy 25 or more options contracts of the same shares, should in case it rises in value. So instead of having to sell part of the 4,000 shares to meet any

assignment received, the trader uses part of the option proceeds to reduce the losses, but if it happens other way round the trader could keep the proceed of the calls that was sold.

Buying puts

A put option contract give the buyer of the contract (who becomes the holder of the contract) the obligation or the right to sell a specified number of shares of the underlying financial instrument (stock, or ETFs shares) at the given strike price on or before the expiration date of the contract.

The reasons for purchasing a put options are discussed below;

1. A trader could buy puts to profit for the anticipated decline in the price of a stock. For example, the shares of Green Mountain Coffee Roasters (GMCR: NASDAQ) has been facing pressure advancing past the $90 a share price, it hit the range twice and with less volume, so a decline was in the horizon. If a trader wanted to profit from the anticipated decline over the next few weeks as we can see from the chart below the trader would purchase puts.

By buying naked puts, just like buying calls for an anticipated upward move of a stock, could be very profitable if the stock moves downwards, this is especially true if you buy an out-of-the-money put options, they could move in such an unbelievable way. When you buy a put it just like a call, only that you are anticipating a fall in the price of the stocks. The money you pay for the put is the maximum you could lose if the share decided to advance in price, but the profit is limitless.

For example, from the GMCR chart above, if in early September 2013 you purchased the GMCR Nov 13: 85 Puts, and as you can see by 23rd of October the share is worth less than $62.5 per share. By doing this you have the right to sell the shares at $85 per share despite its current relative low valuation. So by exercising the option you buying the share for $62.5 on the market and selling it to the seller of the option at $85 per share, before the expiration in November 2013 (that is, the seller of the put is now obliged to take the delivery of the shares at a higher price).

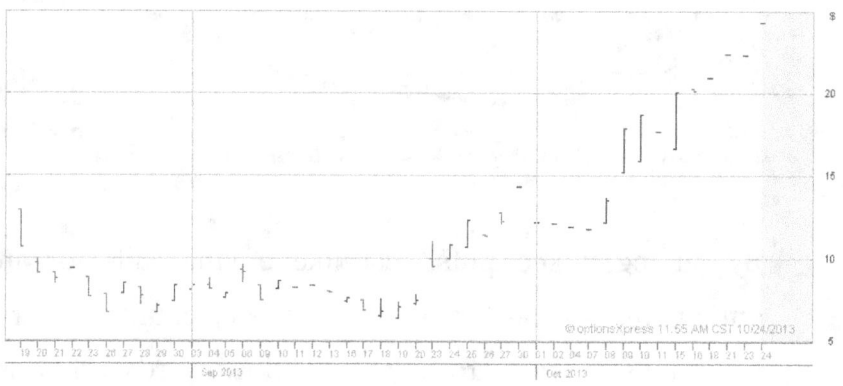

From the chart above, the price of the puts contract was $8.10 early September, and buy October 23 it was worth $23. Therefore, if you bought 40 contracts (4,000 x $8.10= $32,400) and sold at $23 (4,000 x $23= $92,000), profiting $59,600. A whopping 183.95% GAIN, these are the type of options deals you get when you join us at *hiqtraders.com*.

However, another option would be for the holder of the put options to buy the 4,000 shares at $62.5 in the market and then turn around and sell it to the put option writer for $85 (their profit would be $(85-62.5) x 4,000= $90,000), a 36% gain. Apparently, your guess is right as to which option above the put option holder would choose to exercise their rights on the put option contract. This strategy limits the maximum loss the holder of the put would incur thereby allowing them to profit from the decline of the stock price.

2. A trader could buy a put in order to protect themself from a decline in price of a share.

If for example, I have some millions of 'dormant' dollars and I purchased the shares of GMCR at the peak of $87.50 and then found out that I may have purchased them a steep price. I decided that I need to protect myself against a drop in price in the nearest future. What I would then do is to buy puts to protect a long stock position. This strategy is known among the pros popularly as the "married put." So if the stock then falls in price, I would make money on my puts, apparently the profits is minus the premium paid (no matter how far the stock price declines, and because they are my stocks I can easily wait for them to recover in price and resell them later. However, the beauty of this strategy is that it would produce a gain if in the future the stock appreciates more than the cost of the premium paid for the put option.

Look at this way as well, say you bought 100 shares of EBAY for example at $50 per share and, to protect yourself from fall in the price of EBAY you purchased EBAY August 50 put at $1 per contract in premium, a bill of $100. The shares was for a cost of $5,000, by buying these puts it guarantees that no matter how hard the shares price falls you would sell it for $5,000 (or say $50 per share).

Now if the price of the stock moves up to $60 per share and the put premium drops to $0.6, now your EBAY shares are worth $6,000 but our put is now out-of-the-money. If we decided to cash in buy selling our EBAY shares now, our profit would be $900 ($(6000-5000) - $100 cost of the premium).

However, if the EBAY shares fell to $40, then our loss on the shares would be $1,000 and the put options would then be in–the-money so they would be exercised, allowing us to sell the shares for $50, our loss would be cost of the premium paid. But we would have preserved the value of our EBAY shares.

Selling calls

Now let us look at the other side of the trade. When you buy calls you are bullish, remember there is always two sides to a story, and two sides to a coin, there is no market without a buyer and seller, simple. So when you sell calls you are bearish. So you are called the call seller. Almost 80% of the options expire worthless every month, so selling calls could be a great way to collect 'rent' on your shares or just to make money (an alternative to making higher interest on your cash in the bank). Remember monopoly game!

Now hear this, as a call writer you are obliged by the OCC to sell the stock or the underlying shares at the predetermined strike price as agreed by the terms of the call contract whenever you are assigned an exercise notice. For this right or obligation, you are paid a premium by the buyer of the call at the time you sell the call.

a. *Covered Call Writing*

Since selling a call, exposes you to unlimited risk if the share price drops most brokers would not allow you to sell calls without having the commensurate amount of shares in their deposit (i.e. margin) or equal amount of funds available to cover the cost of being assigned at any point. This is called a margin, and you can be called upon to increase it if the market moves adversely against your position, otherwise if you don't answer the margin call the position would be liquidated pronto.

Covered call writing is essentially writing or selling calls against a long position in the underlying stock (that is, shares you own). The idea of writing calls is that the underlying shares would remain stagnant in price or the price falls. Pension funds and corporate investors sell covered calls to earn some money on the shares they own and sometimes to gain some protection (limited to the amount of the premium collect) from a decline in the stock price in their portfolios. If calls are sold uncovered it is a recipe for disaster as any slight positive earnings report on a stock would push its share price through the roof. This is known as *short-squeeze*. I search for it all the time, they are rare opportunity for making money in the market. Short-squeeze skews the market more in favour of the owners of naked calls and puts.

As a call seller your gain is limited to amount of premium that you were paid or you collect on the sale of the call, but your losses could be huge if the share price goes up, it is unlimited.

Essentially, as a covered call writer, you own the underlying stock or have an equivalent funds equal to the value of the underlying shares but you are willing to risk any price increases in excess of the option strike price in return for the premium collected. You must be prepared to deliver the necessary shares of the underlying stock (if and whenever you are assigned) at any time during the life of the option.

Another way out is to of course is to buy calls in the same series at any time prior to being assigned an exercise notice, this allows you to close the transaction with less risk or losses.

If you write a covered call, and then you get assigned it means that your profit or loss is determined by the difference in the amount of the premium you have already collected and the profit make on the calls you bought on the same stock as a hedged-play. The writer would automatically get assigned if the stock price rises above the strike price of the option.

Once the writer of the call is assigned if he has the shares of the underlying stock as his/her margin he would have to sell them (at the strike price, which would definitely be lower than the current market price of the underlying stock) to cover for being assigned. Once he does that he or she forgoes the opportunity to profit from further upward move of the stock price.

On the other hand if the stock price falls, the losses on the shares he hold would be there and the premium collected would be his gain. As soon as call gets assigned it automatically in most cases pushes the shares price of the stock northwards more and even so faster, as the delta on the option increases to 1.

For example, I have 4,000 shares of MNST valued at say $10 per share. I then write calls on them (depositing the shares as margin with my broker), say for MNST May $15 calls at a premium of say $0.3. Four thousand shares equals 40 contracts, therefore I get a total of $1,200 from the sale of the calls as premium ($0.3x 4,000). This income of $1,200 that I described as a 'rent', it is one of the main idea of writing calls making money off the shares you own.

If the stock declines by more than $0.3 then the covered call (essentially a long stock/short call) would show a loss. If the price of the stock falls to say $9, then the paper loss on that stock would be $4,000, the premium collected would reduce the loss to $2,600 on that day, mind you the stock may rebound later, this would be cool for the call writer. The write could close the position (by buying the call, i.e. buy to close trade) as well, and escape being assigned in the future.

However, the share price may go up to $15 which means the writer would get assigned, therefore I would need to sell the share at $ 40,000 (4000 x 10), instead of at $60,000 (4,000 x 15). Therefore, as an option call writer I have forgone that opportunity to sell the share at $15 for a profit, I have only the $40,000 + the $1,200 premium.

What some call writers do is to sell out-of-the-money calls collecting low premiums which in most cases means the risk of them being assigned on the call is very low. Selling in-the-money calls gives the writer more premium but with the higher chance of being assigned easily, except if sharp downturn in the market occurs, as anticipated.

In summary when you write a call, you have decided to forgo any opportunity to profit from an increase in the stock price, having accepted to bear the risk of a drop in the value of your stock holdings, the only gain here is the premium you have collected on the sale of the calls.

b. *Uncovered Call Writing*

A call option writer is uncovered since he does not own the underlying shares of the options sold. The primary aim is to profit from the stock declines. Similar to short selling shares. These kind of trades were common during the recession, when a company shares could be pounced upon by hedge funds and their shares sold short, triggering a run on the particular company's shares and causing further declines. It is a naked position, as you do not have the underlying shares as a back-up. Most brokers would not allow you to trade naked call writing if you do not deposit funds, that is, have money for margin calls with them before you institute these kind of trades. This is to have assurance that the stock can be purchased for delivery if and when assigned.

Selling Puts

Selling a put makes you obliged to buy the shares of an underlying stock at the option's strike price upon assignment of an exercise notice. When you sell a put you receive a premium, this is what you get paid by the buyer of the put, to give that buyer or holder of the put the right to buy the shares cheap when they fall.

The seller of the put expects the shares to rise in value, since at that point the holder or buyer of the put would not want to buy the shares above the strike price, in that case the put would be out-of-the-money. The buyer of the put expects the shares to fall in price, so that the idea is that he or she would exercise that right (the right he purchased by buying the put options) to buy the shares at a discount and resell at a premium in essence making a profit. The put writer must be prepared to buy the underlying stock /or cover the short at any time during the life of the option should he or she get assigned.

a. *Covered Put Writing*

For you to be allowed to sell puts, just like in call writing, you must have the corresponding amount of shares in terms of options contracts, that is, if you sell 40 put contracts of that particular stock, then you should at least 4,000 shares of that stock deposit with your broker. Otherwise you would be required to maintain a margin equivalent to the prices of the stock, and you could be called to deposit more if your positioned is assigned to cover your losses, in the case you could not cover additional margin request, your positions would liquidated to limit your losses. Period.

If you have a corresponding amount of the stock you are shorting, then you have a covered put position (married put). A covered put writer has a limited profit potential, but the put buyer potential for profit is unlimited, with a maximum loss of the premium paid. The maximum gain a put seller has is the premium that he or she has received.

b. *Uncovered Put Writing*

A put writer that does not have corresponding stock position of a stock shorted is uncovered. This is very similar to what happened to mortgage backed securities that were sold pre-recession days. When the prices of real estate collapsed and the securities that were sold short with the believe that prices of real estate would never fall were caught naked when prices fell and the owners of those securities, having paid companies like AIG for the right to sell the properties, by paying AIG premiums, (i.e. their loans or debts) at the pre-recession prices got AIG and others assigned and AIG could not pay out. It was a disaster. This is what happens when you sell shorts and are not covered.

For a put writer if the stock price declines below the strike price of the put, you would get assigned as that must happen, the put seller would then be obliged to pay for the stock at the strike price. Essentially, the holder of the put buys the stock at the fallen current market price and sells it to the seller of the put at the expensive (strike) price.

As an example, if you wrote a put on a stock BNN, that is a BNN August 65 puts for a premium of $2, if the market price of this BNN stock drops from $65 to $55 per share you would get assigned. Then you must buy 100 shares of BNN at a cost of $6,300 ($6,500 to purchase the stock at the strike price minus $200 premium income received).

At time the price of the share, in this case, BNN could drop to $63 (65-2) and the put could still be assigned or the put seller could buy a call of the same strike in the same series to close the trade and limit losses, but the loss would be minimal here. If the price of the BNN share remained at or above the strike price of $65, it is extremely unlikely to get assigned and the $200 collected would be kept as a profit. Even if the holder wants to assign the cost to the brokerage (i.e. commission and fees) to close the trade could be discouraging on an out-of-the-money option.

The primary motivation for most put writers is to receive premium income and acquire stock at a net cost below the current market value. If the stock price rises, the put options would most likely expire.

Call Spreads

A call spread is a type of options strategy whereby the trader buys and sells call options contracts simultaneously in equal numbers on the same stock usually with different strike prices and/or sometimes at different expiration dates. The purpose is to limit the trader's maximum loss but in essence limit their maximum potential profits as well simultaneously.

Put Spreads

A put spread is a type of options strategy whereby the trader buys and sells put options contracts simultaneously in equal numbers on the same stock usually with different strike prices and/or sometimes at different expiration dates. The purpose is to limit the trader's maximum loss but in essence limit their maximum potential profits as well at the same time.

I would talk more about options spreads and how to make money from them in my other book on options, I highlighted how to simply harness the power of spreads to make consistent gains in the market. I can guarantee you that never has options spreads been discussed in such simple details yet powerful enough. It is like a nuclear force, the power that a nucleus possess is so powerful yet it is the smaller part of the cell.

Chapter Three:
Trading Options: Getting Started in Options Trading

Brokerages and Trading Accounts

Now that we have discussed the basics of options trading, we now turn our attention to the trading options. Before you can trade options you would need to open an account with an options broker. Most brokerages now offer options trading. My recommended ones are OptionsXpress, TD Ameritade and Tradeking. As soon you set up your account and it gets approved for trading, which is a simple process, you fund your account and start trading. You would usually in most cases get a tutorial on the workings of the platform of the brokerage, teaching you how to place orders and cancel orders as soon on and so forth, get familiar with your brokers' platform it is very important.

Trading accounts are usually cash or margin accounts. The difference between a cash and margin account is that with a cash account you can only use the available or settled cash in your account to pay for all your stock and/or options trades. On the other hand a margin account is like a credit card, it allows you access to funds that are secured against holdings in your account, typically your existing holdings or some sort of cash facility (e.g. stocks or long-term options) as collateral to borrow funds from the brokerage to finance additional purchases of stocks or options.

Most brokerages do not have a minimum deposit for opening a trading account, however if you want to trade futures contracts or options on futures contracts they may have additional requirements. This additional requirements or margin (usually a minimum deposit) required depends on the type of account that you are opening as well as the brokerage firm. Little or no deposit is required to open a cash account while federal regulations require a deposit of at least $2000 to open a margin-enabled account (always check with your brokers for the current guidelines).

Most brokerages have an online platform, however they would still allow you to place trades via telephone calls if you have a down-time on your internet for example (sometimes for a fee) or via their online chat rooms (accessible from their website, I have done this before when a block on pop-ups on my new laptop prevented me from using my brokers' platform). However, to trade options effectively, I believe a brokerage firm should allow people to place trades online or via mobile phone apps (OptionsXpress and TD Ameritrade have a very simple to use mobile phone apps). In a typical options trades, most especially the complex trades, like the spreads and the condors, I personally believe that there are too many variables unlike the regular stock buy and sell transaction. If I have to communicate all the details of an option spread trade via a simple telephone conversation it could be a hassle, and this could be disastrous depending on the amount involved.

The beauty of a brokerage with an online or mobile phone app / access is that they can handle numerous orders simultaneously without errors, this in turn generates more income for them. Apparently with the ease that online access has brought to trading there appears to be a commensurate increase in the volume of trading, even more for option trades that are processed by the brokers and the exchanges overall.

In the past I have used some options brokers that were quite cheap in terms of commissions that I found that my orders were not filed easily and I did not get good prices with my order fills. Sometimes it is worthwhile to do away with some cash in terms of fees and commissions to guarantee go order entry at the best prices. Some brokers charge you a flat charge for filling your order, for example my broker OptionsXpress charges me $15 commission on each contract filled up to 10 contracts, so if I buy 1 contract or 9 or 10 contracts I pay $15 (+ exchange registration fees).

Some brokers offer you an advisory (full) service in terms what options to buy and sell, and therefore charge you for the trade they enter, either in or out plus the commission and registration fees applicable for each trade, and they may charge a certain fee monthly in conjunction with other charges. Some brokers offer you self-directed service, which is usually discounted.

Discount brokers are usually geared towards the self-directed trader. They usually do not offer investment advice and therefore leave their clients to make their own trade decisions, when they enter and exit a trade, and hence they are much cheaper overall. Some other brokerages offer both services to their clients and would charge their clients on a *pay-as –you-go* basis depending on the service you requested at that point in time. I trade with a discount broker and enter and exit at my call.

Among other factors in choosing a broker, the speed at which they execute their transactions is paramount. To me this is the most important thing in choosing a broker, because they should be able to process large amount of transactions without their systems becoming overwhelmed. My broker offers me options quotes 15 minutes delayed, however I subscribe to stockcharts.com to view live market prices and this helps in my entry and exit orders. Getting some sort of access to live prices is important, you need to know and be able to respond to price quotes as they change. Ensuring you have access to fast connection to the internet is also beneficial. I have made an extra $3,419.23 on a particular trade by having an access to live quotes and a very good internet connection. This happens once a while but when they do you would never regret it, it pays for itself. Trust me!

Commissions and fees

Like I discussed earlier, it is important to know how your brokerage charges commissions and fees on your orders placed. Whenever I trade options via the OptionsXpress I get charged $15 for every option contracts trades up to 10 contracts.

Some brokers charge per trade fee or per contract fee.

Per trade fee is the usual minimum fee charged per transaction, regardless of how many options contracts traded. Per contract fee is the fee is charged by the broker for every option contract that you trade. You could get better discounts if you do frequent trades in a month so always ask you broker for details. Ensure you check if your broker would charge you inactivity fee(s), monthly/annual maintenance fees (whether you trade or not) or minimum balance fees.

Options Chains

				Calls						Puts			
Last	Chg	Bid	Ask	Vol	Opint	Action	▲ Strike ▼	Last	Chg	Bid	Ask	Vol	Opint	Action
		Dec13 Calls		(20 days to expiration)			EXPE @ 63.69							Dec13 Puts
0	0	22.50	24.30	00	0	Trade | Detail	40.00	0.05	0	0	0.05	00	33	Trade | Detail
0	0	21.50	23.30	00	0	Trade | Detail	41.00	0.05	0	0	0.05	00	363	Trade | Detail
0	0	20.90	22.00	00	0	Trade | Detail	42.00	0.03	0	0	0.05	00	118	Trade | Detail
0	0	18.89	20.90	00	0	Trade | Detail	43.00	0.02	0	0	0.05	00	101	Trade | Detail
18.00	0	18.30	20.40	00	0	Trade | Detail	44.00	0.03	0	0	0.05	00	688	Trade | Detail
15.40	0	18.80	20.00	00	0	Trade | Detail	45.00	0.02	0	0	0.05	00	304	Trade | Detail
13.46	0	15.80	16.90	00	0	Trade | Detail	46.00	0.05	0	0	0.05	00	102	Trade | Detail
5.00	0	14.80	17.60	00	0	Trade | Detail	47.00	0.12	0	0	0.05	00	1,313	Trade | Detail
13.36	0	14.20	15.90	00	3	Trade | Detail	48.00	0.10	0	0	0.05	00	1,128	Trade | Detail
13.50	0	14.50	14.00	00	2	Trade | Detail	49.00	0.10	0	0	0.05	00	638	Trade | Detail
11.47	0	13.60	13.80	00	57	Trade | Detail	50.00	0.02	0	0	0.05	00	9,179	Trade | Detail
9.10	0	6.60	8.80	00	6,249	Trade | Detail	55.00	0.05	0	0	0.10	00	9,699	Trade | Detail
4.10	0	4.10	4.40	00	7,565	Trade | Detail	60.00	0.60	0	0.50	0.60	00	4,239	Trade | Detail
1.25	0	1.20	1.25	00	2,238	Trade | Detail	65.00	2.60	0	2.50	2.60	00	466	Trade | Detail
0.15	0	0.15	0.20	00	142	Trade | Detail	70.00	6.70	0	6.40	6.60	00	117	Trade | Detail
0.05	0	0	0.05	00	237	Trade | Detail	75.00	0	0	10.70	11.50	00	0	Trade | Detail
0	0	0	0.05	00	0	Trade | Detail	80.00	17.80	0	16.20	16.40	00	0	Trade | Detail
		Jan14 Calls		(48 days to expiration)			EXPE @ 63.69							Jan14 Puts
		Apr14 Calls		(139 days to expiration)			EXPE @ 63.69							Apr14 Puts
		Jul14 Calls		(230 days to expiration)			EXPE @ 63.69							Jul14 Puts

© OptionsXpress.com 2013.

Options Symbols

When I started trading options in the early 2000's, the symbols for options are usually complex, though with time you get to understand them, but now the symbols are still the same, but what we as traders see is the user-friendly version of the quote. Now it is bliss trading options with the new much easier symbols and codes options symbols are much simpler. I have given a sample of an option contract quote below for MNST: MNST DEC 13 60 CALL $1.10.

The first item, here it is MNST it is the symbol for the stock, it is followed by the month, day and year. This is date the option contract expires, in this example that would be Friday Dec., 20, 2013. The option type is a call with strike price of $60, sold for $1.1 per contract. Simple.

MNST DECEMBER 21, 2013 60 CALL AT $1.10

Or for short, it can be written as
MNST DEC 13 60 CALL $1.10

NB: The option quote above are only written for illustrative purposes only, they should not be construed as a solicitation to trade a specific option. While it may present an actual price quote it is not intended to be so.

Weekly Options

With the introduction of weekly options, every options trader should pay close attention to the option they have selected to trade before clicking the trade confirmation button. Ensure it is the correct Stock, the right expiration month or week, select the desired strike price and whether it is a call or put. If you suspect that you are seeing a cheaper price than expected, then it is probably that you have selected a weekly option, Check the trade one more time, one by one, piece by piece, before clicking that confirmation button.

Last Price

The last price for option price is the last traded price, but this can be misleading, it does not say at what time is was, whether it was 15 minutes ago, an hour or more, etc. Do not think that the 4.39 a.m. (the time at the right end) was the last traded time that time is simply the time the price quote was accessed, in this case at 4.39 a.m. on Saturday, November 30, 2013. Clearly the markets are closed at that point.

© OptionsXpress.com 2013.

To avoid errors with entering your desired option to be traded the best thing is to use the order entry users' interface on your broker's' platform instead on entering it directly in to the order sheet on their platform.

Bid-Ask Spread

This is difference between the bid and ask prices, that is, the difference in the price you sell the option is this context and the price you buy it. Incidentally, the ask price is higher than the bid price. The more narrow the bid-ask spread is the more liquid the financial instrument.

They tend to widen during periods of market volatility as the market makers need to ensure they are covered and they make profits. When the market opens as there could be very few orders coming through (except when a stock releases their earning report at the market closing the day before or it pre-market opening) at those points the spreads could widen due to low market liquidity. Liquidity dictates the bid and ask spreads. As there is more open interest in the options that are in-the-money or options that have strike prices that are very close to the current market price of the stock they tend to have narrower bid-ask spreads. Options with lower the open interest tend to have wider bid-ask spread. Looking at the piece above from OptionsXpress.com the bid-ask spread is $1.05 to $1.1.

Order Entry

I have decided to use another snapshot from optionsXpress.com to illustrate this section. The order entry could be different from this if you are executing a spread. This is what you get when you are trying to enter an order for a straight forward buy for calls or a put. Entering an order is intuitive as you could see from the box below. You simply enter the underlying stock or security symbol, the expiration month/week (if buying weekly options).

Options Order Form

[Screenshot of an options order form with fields: Symbol (EXPE, Dec13, 60, Call), Action (Please Select), Quantity (All or None), Price (Market, Limit $, Stop $, Stop Limit, Market On Close), Duration (Day Order), Advanced Orders (None), with buttons Preview Order, Speed, Save]

© OptionsXpress.com 2013.

In the action box you enter whether you want to buy or sell, and you could choose buy to open and sell to open to open a position. Or select buy to close and sell to close, these are for orders to close a position(s).

Quantity

Here you select the number of option contract/s that you intend to buy. In options trading, each contract represents 100 shares. This is where your fees and commissions are determined. Fees and commissions that you get charged depends on the amount of contract you buy and or sell. Some brokers would give you discounts for larger orders and some would have a minimum commission charge for every order this excludes any applicable discounts in most cases.

All or None Orders

Just as the name suggests, if you select this instruction on your order, the broker would not fill your order except they can guaranteed that all of your orders would be filled. Sometimes if I really want to get in to that particular trade I don't tick this. Otherwise, I could miss out on that golden opportunity. You can only select this order option for limit orders, not when you simultaneously ticked the order to fill at the market price.

Options Trading

In options trading the buyer or seller can exit any position before the expiration date.

If for example, the options buyer buys a call or put to enter a trade, he or she has to sell to close the call or sell to close the puts contracts respectively to close the trade. Similarly, the seller of the call or put must buy the call or put to close the trade as well, if they desire to do so prior to expiration.

I use the OptionsXpress.com trading platform for my options trade, so I would see their platform as I have pictured some of their trade entry snapshots above to describe entering and exiting orders when trading options.

How to Enter an Options Trade:

Buy-to-open

This a transaction where you buy a call or put to open the trade. Essentially, you are long the position. To initiate a naked trade you either buy a call or put to open the trade. Sometimes you could initiate a trade, for example, a spread trade by simultaneously buying and selling a call and put.

Sell-to-open

This a transaction where you sell a call or put to open the trade. Essentially, you are short the position. To initiate this kind of trade it must be covered; either with a spread position where you buy call options on the sold call or vice versa for the puts; or by depositing some equivalent amount of cash that is commensurate with the value of the shorted stocks with the broker.

How to Close an Options Trade:

Buy-to-Close

Once you have a trade open you must close them at some point, except you allow the option contracts to expire worthless. If you sold a call to open the trade you would have to buy it to close that trade, hopefully at a lesser price to make a gain.

This can also be the case when you sold a call to open a trade (or as part of a spread trade) and to close that transaction (earlier before expiration may be to avoid being assigned) or partially close that trade for some other reason you would need to 'buy-to-close' on the 'sell-to-open' part of the spread trade.

Sell-to-Close

To exit a previously opened trade, for example a buy-to-open trade on a call or put, prior to expiration date you would need to sell-to-close the transaction.

Types of Orders

There are many type of orders that you could initiate via the OptionsXpress.com platform and most other platforms are similar. This is to allow a very flexible trading environment for their clients and reduce order enter errors. They include among others; market orders, limit orders and stop orders, as you could see from the OptionsXpress.com options order form above.

Market Order and Limit Orders

What a market order means is that you want to buy or sell the asset, i.e. option, at the current market price. Like I described earlier every asset has two prices, i.e. the bid and the ask price. The ask price is the price you would pay to buy and the bid price is what you pay to sell the asset. The spread between the two is the profit of the market maker(s) whoever they are.

Market order guarantees instantaneous fills of your orders, as you are purchasing at the current market/live price, with the downside of paying more for the asset in most cases, but in a fast moving asset you may need to enter at a higher price before missing out on the opportunity for the price move. I have missed a very profitable trade before because I wanted to enter at a price (by using limiting order) $0.05 less than the current asking price. Sometimes you need to make some little losses to get the bigger slice of the pie.

On the other hand with limit orders you specify to your broker the exact price you would want to purchase or sell an asset for. That is, you would not buy if the price were higher or sell if the price were lower. It gives you the ability to control what your gain is and what you expect to lose of any trade, the downside obviously, as I described above, is that your order may not be filled.

Stop Loss Orders

As the name implies stop loss orders are designed to limit losses on particular trades. You could implement Stop Market Order or a Stop Limit Order. They are executable only if the trader's pre-set price (stop limit loss) gets hit by the market price of the asset or reaches a certain price which is more that than the risk tolerance of the trader (stop market order).

Stop Market Order

It is a stop order which gets executed only if the price of the asset, i.e. option trades lower than or above the market price of the asset. It gets executed if the price of the asset trades lower than its current market price when a trader is in a long position, therefore reduces the loss *(sell stops)*. Or is a trader is in a short position is gets executed if the price of the asset trades higher than its current market price of the asset *(buy stops)*.

Like the market orders described in the previous section, in volatile trading environments the actual filled price for that stop market order trade may be different from that set by the trader, it may be higher for buy stops or lower for sell stops, especially when market prices gaps, but the good thing about it is that you are almost guaranteed a fill.

Stop Limit Order

This is another type of stop loss order which gets activated only when the asset price falls or goes above a pre-set price by the trader. It gives the trader the ability to predict his or her maximum loss. The downside is that is only executed when that set target price is reached.

National Best Bid or Offer (NBBO):

The National Best Bid or Offer (NBBO) is an Securities and Exchange Commission (SEC) requirement that brokers must guarantee customers the best available ask price when they buy securities and sell securities. Look for brokers that guarantee trade execution prices that meet or exceed the NBBO.

Put-Call Ratio

I am not going to go in to the details of how the put-call ratio is calculated. First of all, I would tell you about it, obviously making you realise that it exists, and then I would discuss the application of it. Simply put, the put-call ratio is the total number of puts options traded divided by the total number of call options traded at a given period.

Most traders naturally believe that the share price would always go up, and they are right, in most cases the share prices of most stocks would go up eventually, despite some significant setbacks during recession or economic crises. Now this assumption skews the price of stock options. In the short term stock prices rises and falls and since options contracts are decaying assets/derivatives, time does not favour the buyer of the call or put options. And since there are more buyers than sellers in probability profit terms the sellers have more short term advantage at making money by selling options.

Therefore, put-call ratios (PCR) are never 1, since more calls are purchased relative to puts, then the PCR is usually less than 1, when it is more than 1 it means the overall market is pessimistic. PCR is usually around 0.35 – 0.95, with the typical range at or about 0.6-0.7. There are different types of PCRs which I would discuss shortly.

When a PCR value is <1 it usually indicates a bearish bias in the market. When it is higher especially if it increasing it indicates a shift in market sentiment to a negative one. In most cases, usually often than not a value of ≤0.5 is a bullish market bias.

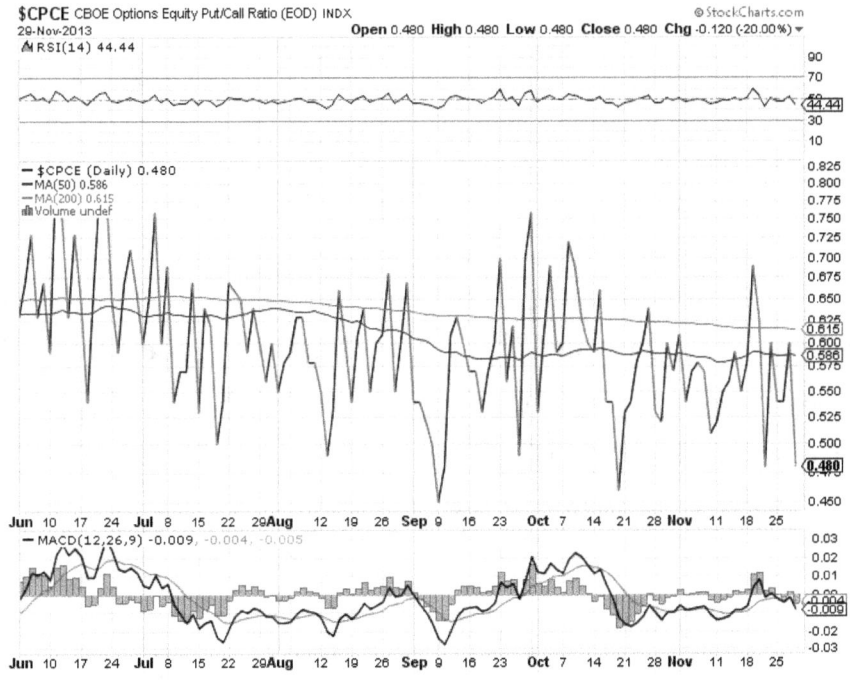

Contrarian traders use the PCR as an indicator most especially to determine when the markets or the investing public are getting too excited positively or afraid scared to invest. So therefore for a contrarian a high PCR is a bullish sign as the it points to an over-bearish crowd, and the same goes for the a low PCR which would mean an over-bullish crowd for the contrarian investor.

I use Stockcharts.com for my daily market analysis, because it is simple and straight forward to use. In stockcharts.com there are five different put/call Ratios provided for analysis. The CBOE divides their analysis in to three figures and we have two more, that is, from the PSE options put/call ratio and the Philadelphia options put/call ratio.[24]

The Chicago Board Options Exchange (CBOE) is the biggest hence their figures are usually widely watched, and it broken down in to three groups: equity, index and total that is the CBOE Equity Put/Call Ratio, CBOE Index Put/Call Ratio and the CBOE Total Put/Call Ratio.

The CBOE Equity Put/Call Ratio ($CPCE) focuses on options traded on individual stocks. The CBOE Index Put/Call Ratio ($CPCI) focuses on options traded on the major indices, such as the Dow, Nasdaq, Russell 2000, S&P 500 and S&P 100. Equity and index options are combined with the CBOE Total Put/Call Ratio ($CPC).[24]

The important idea here is that the CBOE gives the CBOE Equity Put/Call Ratio and the CBOE Index Put/Call Ratio for a reason. The hedge managers/guys, do a job of protecting their assets that is why it is called hedge funds, by buying index put options. Therefore one would expect the PCR of the index options to be much higher than for the equity options, as they would sell more puts on the assets under their management. In essence, the equity put call ratio is used to give a better indicator of the investing crowd.

LEAPS® which means Long-term Equity Anticipation Securities, they are a special kind of options, and they are available for long-term stock or index options that are scheduled to expire more than 9 months in advance, and they could be available for up to 2-3 years ahead. I must tell you that they are slightly more expensive that the regular options, but much cheaper than their underlying stocks.

They are used to get access to inherent opportunities in to a stock that has the potential to become a winner in about twelve to thirty-six months time, it offers all the advantages of a typically option, providing leverage and downside protection. For good LEAPS® that do move high as anticipated the return on investment could be in excess of over 2,000%. However, I would need to tell you that the market for LEAPS® are usually available for the most commonly traded and popular stocks, which could be an advantage, but the main idea of the LEAPS® is forfeited because it should give you a 'cheap' entry to a potential future winner which is slightly of a higher price. Unfortunately since most of the stocks that have the potential to make a significant upward move in the future are currently in the small or mid cap range LEAPS® are usually not available for them.

Chapter Four:
Options Greeks

One of the things that comes to my mind when I started trading options was the fact that options are highly leveraged instruments and they move up in such a way that it produces massive gains compared to the underlying stocks. For example, when an underlying stock increases from $90 to $92.5, one of its option may move from $0.2 to $1.25,the option price move was larger in terms of percentage price increase, so the next question is, is there a way you could predict all these moves? The answer to that question is YES- *the options Greeks! You do not expect the price of an option to move by $1 for every dollar move in the price of the stock, do you? No, not in all cases!*

The rate of change in the price of an option is determined by some numbers (which are described by Greek alphabets) that have been mathematically derived, they are called Greeks, simply because the Greek alphabets are used to describe them.

For you to successfully trade options you need to constantly access your trading positions regularly to determine the rate of change of your current option price in light of the movement of the price of the underlying stocks. Making money in options is not just buying low to sell high alone, but you should constantly re-assess your positions based on their options Greeks. The Greeks are basically indicators of the predicted price moves of an option based on the options components.

The most common options Greeks are; *Delta, Gamma, Theta, Vega, Rho and the Beta.* I would discuss them one by one, I would try and explain how they are applied as well.

Delta

This is a measure of how sensitive the price of the option is to the change in the price of the underlying asset. For example, if a call option has a delta of 0.5, it means that for every $1 move (up or down) in the price of the underlying stock the option price would gain or lose $0.50 respectively. On the other hand for puts, they have deltas that are negative in value. So if an option has a delta of -0.5 that means for every $1 rise in the value of the stock the value of the put option would fall by $0.5 and if the stock falls by $1 then the value of the put option would rise by $0.5. Calls have positive delta values and they range between 0 and 1 and puts have a negative delta ranging between 0 and -1. I have found out that in-the-money options usually move faster in price than the out-of-the-money options (because they have deltas that are higher in value), but I have preference for the out-of-the-money options because from experience when they are selected properly whenever they move in response to a rapid jump in stock price, the percentage gain compared to the in-the-money options is outrageous!

Though this book was not written specifically for weekly options, but shorter term options like weekly options do react more than options with expiration further down the line.

Traders must monitor the delta value of their options as they constantly change depending on the price of the underlying asset. For example, if a stock is trading at say $95, the 95 calls would be at-the-money and in most cases their delta values would be 0.5. If the stock price drops to $90, then the 90 calls options would now be in-the-money so its delta would drop now to about 0.5, as it was previously deep-in-the-money. The delta value of the 95 calls options would drop in value. Knowing the delta value of your positions is especially important when you are trading spreads, as you would want to ensure that you are trading delta neutral strategies, and as the delta keeps changing you would want to reassess your positions or add positions to maintain delta neutrality.

What you need to remember is that At-the-Money (ATM) options will have a Delta of about 0.5. Deep In-the-Money (ITM) options will have higher delta values. In the case of puts, they have higher negative values; deep out-of-the-money (OTM) options will have lower delta values, and these would be lower negative values for puts.

Deltas for options that are in-the-money calls would move closer to 1 as expiration day gets closer, and for out-of-the-money calls they would approach 0 as expiration gets closer, because as expiration approaches the stock will have less time to move above or below the strike price for your option. The same goes for puts, the delta for in-the-money puts will approach -1 and delta for out-of-the-money puts will approach 0 as expiration day approaches. Some trader do refer to delta with 0.5 as having 50 probability of having a certain price, it all means the same as described above.

In summary, delta can be seen as the chances that an option would be in-the-money, as it is amount an option price will move based on a $1 change in the underlying stock, it always changes daily or say frequently according to the price of the underlying stock.

Gamma

Gamma is the rate of change in the value of the delta of an option as the price of the stock changes. Gamma is what gives you the idea of the rate of possible change in the value of the delta or say, Gamma is the Delta of the Delta. Therefore, if the call options has a gamma value of 0.07, and a delta value of 0.63, then if the stock price moves by $1, the option would gain 0.63 in value and the delta would now be 0.7. If the stock moves again by another $1, then the option price would now move by $0.7 and so on and so forth. When traders use this idea of the gamma moves to determine when to enter and exit options trades, they call these strategies- gamma trading strategies. Options with the highest gamma respond more to changes in the price of the underlying stock.

Theta

Remember I said earlier, that as the option contract approaches expiration day it loses value because seriously who wants to buy an option with no value very close to the expiration day as it appears that it would possibly go unexercised. For calls and puts sellers, the theta is important because they want the option contracts they have sold to expire worthless. Therefore, theta is the rate at which an option loses value as time passes.

Just like a radioactive material, actually I see options as radioactive materials, theta is the *decay factor of an option.* For example, an options with a theta value of $0.01 would lose $0.01 in value as every day passes, therefore the price of the stock does not even have to move for this to be, but in reality the price of a stock is never static during trading so theta keeps changing. The purpose of knowing the theta value of an option before you buy or sell options is that you want to get value for money. An option buyer would go for options with lower theta values and an option seller would want to or prefer to sell options with a higher theta value. This is because a buyer would not want to hold an option which loses value too rapidly and a seller would want to sell an option that loses value rapidly.

Vega (sometimes referred to as Kappa):

Vega is the amount the call and put prices will change, for each corresponding one-point change in implied volatility of the option. When anticipating a major move in the price of a stock I pay close attention to this greek, it can help in defining exits to capture some significant profits and avoid losses of the same magnitude as well.

An option with a Vega of 0.25 will gain $0.25 with a percentage point increase in volatility. For example, if the price of an option is $1.50 with volatility at 20%, then it will have a theoretical value of $1.75 at a volatility of 21% and a value of $1.25 at a volatility of 19%. Therefore, as the implied volatility increases, the value of options will increase; increase in implied volatility indicates that there is an inherent possibility for the price of the stock to increase or decrease in value. In summary, with every point move from say 20% to

19% in the value of the implied volatility, the value of the option changes by $0.25.

Rho

Remember one of the components of time value is interest rates. Rho deals with the role of the current interest rates on the price of the options. In most cases, the prices of call options would increase in value when the interest rate increases, on the other hand put options will decrease in value. The further away in time the options expiration is, the more the impact of the interest rate on the value of the call option, hence the call option value increases. For put options the further away in time the expiration of the put option the more the negative impact of rho on its price. Imagine it this way, the put writer is being lent money, so the writer pays interest on the money collected.

In summary, the greater the options' expiration time frame, the greater the Rho. Rho is the amount an option value will change in theory based on a one percentage-point change in the current interest rate. Since interest rate is about time, as I said earlier that the further the option is from expiration the more the impact of the rho on the option pricing, hence rho has more impact when trading LEAPS due to the greater effect on the cost to carry the options. The effect of rho on shorter-term options trading is quite limited, and it does not affect the value of the option significantly to warrant any much concern.

Beta

This measures the rate of change in the price of an option in response to the changes in the overall market sentiment. Beta is always the reference of the option to a broad market index, it could be the S&P for example. For example, if the beta of the Dow Industrial Average is 1, then the stock with a beta of 1 would be more likely to move with the same volatility as the Dow Industrial Average Index. In a similar vein, a stock with a beta less than 1 will tend to rise and fall not as fast in respect to moves in the Dow Industrial Average Index.

An important thing about beta is that *low beta does not mean low volatility,* and this has nothing to do with the risk on a stock. *Low beta does not mean low risk.* Lots traders even the experts get this wrong. As I described above, beta is about correlation of a stock and its option to another broad market index. Typically, it is that of correlation to the S&P 500 for the past 30 trading days. For example the SPY has a beta of 1.00. The SPY is an ETF that resembles the S&P 500, we shall discuss this in subsequent chapters.

Beware, there could be a slight period in time when the two do not correlate, but they do re-align. If a stock has a beta of 2 that would simply mean that this stock moves twice as much in value with every moves in the same direction as the S&P, and the reverse is the same as well. This is the case for leveraged ETFs which strive to reproduce multiple gain on the move of a particular market index daily.

Like inverse leveraged ETFs which can move south twice/thrice the rate of fall in the price of the underlying index, therefore beta can have negative numbers. Low beta stocks can, and often do, have high volatility. For example over the last 12 months GMCR has been a volatile stock in terms of historical volatility, but it was a high beta stock. Beta is only an indication of the correlation to an underlying index. A low beta stock does not necessarily mean low volatility.

Chapter Five:
Effect of Dividends on Option Pricing

The value of an option is determined by some set of complicated formulas which I would not discussed here, I would only discuss what is relevant. There are some variables, that is, the price of the underlying stock price, volatility, time, dividends and interest rates that determine the 'fair value' of stock options. The last two variables, i.e. dividends and interest rates are very crucial in determining and understanding when to exercise an option.

Dividends (cash dividends) from time to time would have an impact on the price of options, because dividends are priced-in into the value to the option price. Usually the underlying stock price is expected to drop by the cash amount of the dividend on the ex-dividend date. Since options are speculative instruments, the value of the dividends are usually speculated to be such and such amount prior to their release, so they are priced into the value of the option in anticipation that it would be x amount.

If the amount of dividend that is expected to be paid on a stock is larger than the market anticipated, in most cases the value of the stock price would increase, as the market has already priced in that amount the shareholders would receive following dividend payments. If the amount dividend expected to be paid is less than the value the market anticipated then the value of the stock would drop.

This is to say that once a high cash premium is paid, the value of the stock is expected to fall, so in anticipation of this event occurring put options on such stocks are priced higher prior to the ex-dividend date. Most stocks usually drop in value after the ex-dividend date.

Dividend is essentially the amount of cash (sometimes it could come as a stock split; technically, it is not a dividend as the price of the stock reacts to split in different way) that a company pays its shareholders following a period of positive earnings, for the company. Not all stock pay dividends, and not all dividend paying stocks pay dividends all the time. Dividends are usually paid after a shareholder meeting with all stakeholders agreeing or not agreeing to this resolution. Most companies pay dividends quarterly. The amount of dividend a shareholder receives is directly proportional to his or her amount of shares held in the company.

As I described above, the relationship between the move on the stock price and dividend payments is anticipation. Once the dividend amount has been paid, the value of the stock options drop following the ex-dividend date, this is because the value of the dividend as we now see is no longer a factor in the price of the stock. Therefore, the boost in the price of a stock prior to the dividend payment date is a *temporary effect.*

Effects of Dividends on Call & Put Option Pricing

The call options seller is assumed to have collected the dividend of a dividend-paying stock, so these call options are assumed to have been discounted by as much as the dividend amount to be paid. Remember for you to get a dividend from the dividend paying stock you must own the stock by the end of the ex-dividend date.

Therefore, since the seller of the call options is deemed to have received the dividend prior to the ex-dividend date, if a call holder exercises his/her right on the call options he/she receives the dividend from the call options seller. So essentially if you sold a call options prior to ex-dividend date you run the risk of being assigned and paying the dividend after the ex-dividend date. The way out of this for the call options seller to buy-to-close (if there was any profit on the trade) any sell-to-open contracts (buy-to-close on the already sold call options contracts) if you think there is a risk of being assigned. You would know this if the stock gaps up while expecting the dividend value to be announced.

If a high cash dividends is anticipated then it would usually imply lower call premiums and higher put premiums, and vice versa, but remember the market can be irrational at times. After the ex-dividend dates since the value of the stock would drop by the amount of the dividend- put options would get expensive.

How to Play Earnings Report

On way to trade in anticipation of stock earnings release is to buy straddles. The fact is that most times the earnings report on a stock are often unpredictable, but also the beauty of this is the volatility created when the stock gaps up or down in such wide range that missing this kind of opportunity could be painful. Now the best way to make money from an earnings report is to buy a cheap OTM calls, say for about $0.5 and watch it rocket up to something like $2.0 (not unusual). The challenge is that it is often a hit-and-miss approach, but I have been fortunate to hit 80/20 with this approach.

Now for the conservative traders, a better way out is to use straddles. We are well aware that sometimes a good earnings report can trigger a sell off on a stock, especially in cases where investors expected a better result.

To make money from a straddle play prior to earnings, they key thing is that a significant price movement must be expected on the stock for the straddle to be profitable. I usually buy straddles about 5 to 14 trading days prior to the anticipated earnings report, especially for stocks that display historically price swings prior to earning reports, like the GMCR and CREE. Do not buy in to straddle like few days in to earnings, the options prices are usually skewed, or manipulated by market makers at that stage.

At times prior to the earnings report itself, due to the anticipated stock price movements you could exit your trades with a small profit, and watch from the side-lines for another opportunity for re-entry. It is not unusual for the price of a stock to gap up or down from 4% to 15% following the release of the expected earnings report, it is very rare for the price of the stock to remain the same after the anticipated earnings release.

I have seen cases where the news and media are bombarded by the hedge funds 'guys' making jibes pre-earnings report release or a profit warning to be issued by the company or some analysts causing movements (in most cases downwards) on the stock could give an 'early-riser' a quick profit to exit the trade in time. So when playing straddles for earnings report keep your eyes on the price, news and institutional investors.

On the ex-dividend date whoever owns the stock gets paid the dividend on a dividend paying stock. Therefore, most calls that are in the money would get assigned the day before the dividend, so as to get the extra cash dividend, wouldn't you? If you are a call option seller, the best thing is to close your position, minimise your losses on that, and at least avoid the extra pain of having to pay the dividend to the call option owner after you have already incurred losses on the options sale itself. Or if you own a covered call, you could sell your in-the-money calls and use to proceeds to settle the short calls.

The Importance of Ex-dividend Dates

Whenever you use option strategies with short calls or short puts then I would advise you from experience to pay close attention to ex-dividend dates. It happened to me before, I was called by my broker that I owed them some money. I was like how can I owe you money on trade I have already closed. Apparently I close the trade after the post-dividend.

If you do not want to have any unexpected surprises read this part carefully. Once a share goes ex-dividend (that is, essentially the next day after the dividend date, the risk of the options, especially call options, being assigned is extremely high. This is so because if the owner of the call options exercise the day before the ex-dividend date he or she becomes the owner of this stock on record when the dividend is paid, so this is important.

This is usually the case if the call option is in-the-money and the value of the dividend paid is more than the remaining time value in the option. To avoid being assigned this way and end up paying the dividend to the broker (they would ask you to pay it via check or whatever means even if you do not have any funds in your account, it has happened to me before). The best way is for you to roll over your position in the next month or months ahead by buying back your position (in most cases it would be a covered call) and then re-selling another call (again for safety reasons another covered call with a strike price that is out-of -the money). In most of the cases the time value on an options with a later expiration would more likely than not be more than the dividend amount, and thus avoid the risk of early assignment.

Remember this if nothing else, if you are trading with strategies involving shorting calls you should aware of this otherwise you should re-evaluate why you are in the game. When shorting calls, for example covered calls, naked calls, call spreads or short straddles, whenever the options are in-the-money and expiration approaches you would be assigned early and it is most likely to happen a day before the stock goes ex-dividend.

For sellers of put options (*uncovered* (naked) puts, *covered* puts, *put spreads* or *short straddles*) they run the risk of being assigned on the ex-dividend date if these sold put options goes in-the-money days before the ex-dividend date.

For the index options early assignment is not usually a risk, and the same applies to stocks of shares that do not pay dividends. For you to know stocks that do pay dividend, call your broker or you can simply find out by reading about this company on the research section of most brokers' platform.

Paying attention to ex-dividend dates cannot be over-emphasised. If you are a trader of options and you sell covered calls, uncovered or naked seller, sells straddles and or call spread, etc., you should pay close attention to dividends and their dates, and if you are dealing with very illiquid stocks then run away from ex-dividend dates.

I have pasted a snapshot of the Stock Quote detail of CREE, Inc. from my optionsxpress window, these are the kind of information you need.

Earnings Information (per share)		Dividend Information		Option Statistics (CREE)	
Surprise %	-6.25	Underlying currently doesn't pay a dividend.		Today's Option Volume*	4,038
Last Quarter Earnings	0.32			Avg Option Volume	9,845
Next Earnings Date	01/28/2014			Open Interest*	184,725
Next Quarter Earnings Projection	0.32			Avg Open Interest	180,452
Next Year EPS Projection	1.95			Avg Put Call Ratio	1
				Historic Volatility (30 day)	26.82
				Put Call Ratio	0.59

Snapshot of the a section of the Stock Quote Detail of CREE from OptionsXpress.com© OptionsXpress.com. 2013

When to exercise a Put Option

Interest rates are essential in determining when to exercise options, especially put options. An increase in interest rates will drive up the price of calls and cause the prices of puts to fall. In reality it costs less to buy call or put options, so a trader would be more willing to buy call options in an environment with high interest rates.

The best time to exercise a put option is difficult to know, but it is a good time to exercise when the interest that could potentially be earned when a stock is sold at its *strike price* is large enough or when the theoretical value of the options is at parity and its delta is exactly 100.

Stock Splits

Stock split happen for numerous reasons. In a nutshell, it is simply like this, a stock worth say $30 with total of 1 million shares splits in to a 2 for 1, that is for every 1 shares of the stock 1 new one is created, you get one extra share. Therefore, the share price would drop to $15 and there would be 2 million new shares. In this case, 100 shares splits to 200 shares, however the share price is cut in half. Therefore, the net asset value of the company does not changed, the only change is the numbers of outstanding shares.

From experience, when most share prices soar past the $75 mark they could potentially reach the $100 mark in a relatively short span of time. Once you start to see this trend you should be on the lookout for stock splits and be ready to profit from them. The other reason for stock splits would be discussed later in this book.

Most veteran traders are aware that once a stock exhibits this patterns in most cases a stock split of the order of 2-for-1 and sometimes 3-for-2 could be about to take place in the boardroom. Typically, split ratios are 2-for -1; 3-for -1; 3-for-2 and 5-for-2.

When a stock split occurs like in our example above, something interesting happens in the stock options as well. If I have 20 contracts of MELI Oct 2013 call and a stock splits of 2-for-1 occurs, then my number of calls goes up to 40 contracts of the same MELI options, this done on a split-adjusted basis.

Once this happens all the strike symbols are adjusted, you do not need to worry about this as it taken care of automatically by your options brokers, they would list your current holdings under the new symbol (i.e. strike prices etc.).

When there is a consistent increase in the value of a share it is common to see stock splits year after year. Some shares have had about 2-3 splits in 6 years. The exchange have not set any concrete rules as to when a stock split should occur, it is up to the management board as to whether is stock split should or should not occur.

Now from the view point of traders, which I am one obviously, if I want to buy a share and it worth $200, and they announce a stock split, and it drops to $100 there would be more shares available to buy, that is more liquidity, now I can afford to buy more of that company's shares, I see the move as good for me from a traders' perspective.

Is a stock split a good thing?

As we all agree the devil in the details. For you to make a judgement whether a stock split is right thing or not, and whether you should enter in to a trade in anticipation of a split is very "dicey".

If a particular stock has got good fundamentals and its increase in price would in most justify a stock split, however if the fundamentals are woeful, a stock split could be seen or regarded as panic reaction from the board. Often times I have seen that when a split occurs with a run in the price of a stock, the trend would usually continue that way after the split. When this pattern is seen, then it is often a positive one.

Sometimes, you could say a 2-for-1 split, which is that you get 1 new share you every share you hold essentially means you get a 100% dividend, and in the same way a 3-for-2 split is a 50% stock dividend, here the shareholders would receive and extra share for each two shares they own.

Reverse Stock Splits

Some companies could do a reverse stock split, for example after the recent mortgage and global economic crisis of 2006/8 settled, Citibank® fell to from its peak of about $531 per share to less than $10 on May 5, 2009 [20], and there a rumour or fact that NYSE was strongly considering delisting the financial giant from the exchange.

So Citigroup Inc. announced a 1-for-10 reverse stock split of Citigroup common stock and they made proposition to reinstate a quarterly dividend of $0.01 per common share in the second quarter of 2011, which is to be effective from the date of the reverse stock split [5].

Remember that at some point Citibank was once the world's largest bank by market value by its numerous outfits and operations in more than 100 countries. Following a barrage of abysmal losses investors lost all confidence in this financial behemoth, with some having the opinion that it could not restored to health after $37.5 billion losses in a span of about 15 months only[20].

Reverse stock splits are sometimes done to redeem a company's image, like in the case of Citibank, from one of a low priced stock to more highly priced one, and like in the case of Citibank to avoid being delisted from the exchange of course. For example, a 1-to-5 reverse split of a stock at $1 means that the shareholders would receive one share at $5 in exchange for every 5 shares they have at the current price of $1.

Again in the Citibank example, a reverse split of 1-for-10 at $1 would mean that the shareholders would receive one share at $10 in exchange for every 10 shares they have at the current price of $1. Just like in stock split the value of the company does not change in reverse stock splits, the only thing that changes is the number of shares. Period.

In my experience trading options, especially call options, I have found out that stock split and reverse stock splits usually push the price of a stock northwards, and also the price of its calls in a similar direction. This is because traders perceive it as an opportunity to enter a trade in a well-liked shares of a stock that has become really expensive, as it is now affordable for them, therefore acquire a stake the current cheaper price, remember in trading everything is relative to something. A reverse stock split can therefore raise the price of a stock.

On the other hand, a reverse stock split is an effort to raise the price of a stock that has become too "cheap." By lifting the price of a stock via a reverse stock split, it may help attract the attention of investors as well positively. So watch for an impending stock split, it could be another opportunity for you. As at the time of writing, I think the shares of *Google*® and *Priceline*® are ripe for a split.

The reason for my believe that stock and options react favourably to splits is because since the value in dollar terms of the shares drops post-split a small change in the value of the underlying stock would have a proportionally larger change in the value of the options. The usual disadvantage is since the quantity of the contracts you hold increases the commissions you would pay to the brokers increase, but this not significant compared to the profit you stand to gain when the options are exercised.

Chapter Six: Advantages of Options Trading

The volume of options contracts traded in the U.S. exchanges has grown in leaps and bounds really over the last decade, this increase are due to the explosive growth in online trading, reduced transaction costs, quick order fills, exchanges and brokers developing platforms that can handle numerous trades, more intuitive platforms, and mobile trading, and more transparency in the way options contracts orders are exchanged. Options trading has been truly a blessing to the world of trading.

Recent data by the Options Industry Council suggested that the total volume of options contracts traded on U.S. exchanges in 1999 was about 507 million and by 2007, that number had grown to an all-time record of more than 3 billion[10]. Also the average daily volume in SPX weekly options has grown from 13,765 contracts in September 2010 to 179,437 contracts in September 2013 (an increase of 1,204%)[4]. The reasons behind these explosion in option trading is what I am going to discuss in this chapter.

Contrary to popular opinion that options trading is risky, actually they are not, at least compared to what they used to be, if that would be of any consolation to those who have had bad experiences in the past. Saying options are risky means you do not understand or know how to use them. I would discuss the advantages of options trading to an investor and by the time you finish this chapter may be I would have been successful to change your perception on options trading.

Why trade options?

Why trade options? Simple, because it costs less compared to the expected return on investment. For example, you bought a typical option contract @ $0.3 and resold at $2.35 that is a minimum of 680% gain compared to you buying the stock @ $45 and reselling at $48, a 6.66% gain. All excluding brokerages fees and taxes.

I am going to itemise and discuss some of the advantages of trading options in this chapter, so that you know the beauty and benefit of what you are getting into.

1. *Options are really a cost effective derivative for a making profits.*

   As described in the example above, instead of purchasing a 1,000 shares of this stock (@$45 per share) for

$45,000, I could simply buy 10 contracts (which gives me the leverage power to control 1,000 shares of that stock like I would do if I have the purchased the original stock) for $300, all excluding brokerages fees and taxes. Now if I do this I would have extra $42,000 to do other trades, or look for other lucrative opportunities in the market to put my extra cash to work. Isn't that great! And clearly, it is cost efficient, however if the options expired worthless, then it is only a small dent to my trading capital. I can easily move on to better opportunities at least, instead of tying down the whole $45,000 to one single trade, ridiculous!

Clearly, I would need to pick the right stock, right options (i.e. calls or puts), the right expiration month and the strike price. Yes, but there are ways to that.

2.   *Leverage*

Another great benefit of options trading as we have discussed elsewhere is the power of leverage. Nowhere in the trading world can you compare the power of leverage in options trading. Even as great as forex is, it is so volatile and sometimes unpredictable. Now the introductions of options on stocks, ETFs, commodities of all sorts, even forex trading has changed the landscape, increasing liquidity, reducing risks, and increasing gains and leverage. I would restrict myself to discussions on stock and ETFs options trading.

Leverage as it is described means when the right to a return on particular investment is proportionally larger than the initial investment amount. This is what you get in options trading. Recap the example I gave you a 680% return compared to 6.66% returns on the same trade.

A trader bought 10 contracts of Macy (Federated Stores) calls for $0.2 and resold for $2.1 in 2007 for example, whereas the stock itself increased from $38 to $42 a share. That was a 950% gain compared to a 10.5% gains. This is simply creating the potential for bigger gains by using a smaller amount of trading capital. You would be really out of your mind to trade the underlying stocks wouldn't you? That is leverage! It is making your money work *harder* for you. It is not scam!

3. *Hedging*

Now that you have read the two benefits of options trading, you are wondering what hedging means, aren't you?

Now hedging is used in trading various financial assets, whether stocks, ETFs, commodities, forex trading, bonds, forward contracts, futures, currency swaps and interest rates. A hedge as the name implies is a 'safe zone'. It creates an investment position with the intent to buffer against potential losses that may be incurred by a position in an underlying investment; it helps to reduces losses in any open trade.

Option trading can give you this safety, you can use options to provide a hedge for your investments.

Back to our earlier example, you bought a typical option contract @ $0.3 and resold at $2.35 that is a minimum of 680% gain compared to you buying the stock @ $45 and reselling at $48, a 6.66% gain (all excluding brokerages fees and taxes right). So what of if you the share price fell? Now hedging can work both ways depending on what you are anticipating.

For example, you could be expecting a drop in the price of the share or may be a rise. If the price of the stock fell from $38 to $34, that would have been a loss of $4,000 on that trade, however the call options you bought would have been allowed to expire worthless following the drop in stock price value limiting your losses to the $200 invested to buy the options contracts in the first place.

Let us say for example, you own this particular stock in your portfolio, you have spent approximately $45,000 to acquire it which is considerable amount of money depending on your overall financial status. You would want to protect yourself and your investment. Apparently you bought the shares of this stock in anticipation of a future appreciation in price. What of if it drops in value? How can you protect against that....*you buy put options.*

So I would purchase put options on this stock; if the price is currently at $45 and I anticipate that over the next 2 months due to market volatility the price might drop, (with the believe that a drop in the price of the stock would recover later in the nearest future). I could purchase a put option expiring in 7 weeks for example at $0.6. If in deed the market turns south, the price of the put options could typically move to $1.8 at 200% gain. In future the price of the stock could recover and I would have made some extra cash. This is one way to hedge.

Simply put hedging means establishing a position in one market to reduce or buffer losses from exposure to a possible drop in the asset value of offset of another financial security, and as you can see for a small amount of money you can purchase options against to offset a fall in value of our stock position, this can be used for other financial instruments as well.

4. *Less Commissions*

These days various brokerages, offer access to trading your accounts online. Since you trade your account yourself, i.e. self-invest, you get to pay less commissions on your trades and they even ensure you get the best market quote. I can go on and on discussing the benefits of trading online. The beauty of trading options, whether on stocks or ETFs, is that the commissions you pay are much lower compared to trading stocks.

MAKE MONEY CONSISTENTLY TRADING OPTIONS

5. *Less Risk*

Clearly, I have described in the first and second chapters of this book that you could purchase an option for $400 and resell them in 4 days for $2,500 and bag a profit of $2,100. This is not once-in-a-while profit we see this frequently. This is a 525% profit. However, if the options expired worthless, you stand to lose only a maximum of $400. Now sit back, look at it again, you are risking $400 to make at least $2,100 profit or more. What kind of investment or trading opportunity gives you so much leverage and *less risk today*? In fact I would should how to risk less to even make more by trading ETFs. Join our exclusive membership group at betaptionsignals.com and I would show you how.

6. *Trading up. Down and Sideways*

Traditionally when you trade stocks, you either bullish or bearish. You never had the option to profit from the stock by being bullish-and-bearish at the same time. Now options gives you that choice. You can structure an options trade on a stock whereby you buy a call and sell a call on the same options series. Or you buy a call, sell a call, and then buy a put and sell a put on the same stock with the same option series.

These kind of spreads gives you the opportunity to profit from the stocks, ETFs, currencies ETFs, indices and anything tradable even if you do not know where the market is heading. Doing this you makes money in the market even when it appears there is no money to be made.

7. *Income*

Options also offers some income generating capability for the sellers. Like I described in the book much earlier, that if I own such an x amount of shares on a stock, I could sell options on them, for example call options, in anticipation that the price of the stock would fall. By collecting this premium from the buyer, I am invariably collecting 'rent' on my stocks or income or let's say a 'dividend' on it.

8. *Indices*

In the past there was no way you could trade the index on the markets, indices like the Dow Jones Industrials, Standard and Poor's, the Russells, and the Nasdaqs. They were untradeable. Now with the advent of the ETFs and now options on ETFs they are traded like any normal stock. Traders can now trade the movement of the overall broad indices on the markets and take advantage of price changes.

9. *Opportunity*

Options has opened up new and various methods, including opportunities in trading today. Options are available on stocks, ETFs, currencies, bonds and interest rates. You name it there a stock or index on these and much more that you could trade options on.

10. Liquidity

One of the attractions as I have discussed in options trading is that you do not tie too much of your capital down on a trade. You pay so much to buy only few shares of a stock, but you could control the same number of shares on this stock with little money down. Options are very liquid, most stocks that have options available on them are very liquid, as they must pass some set of criteria before are allowed to be traded on them.

11. Price Availability

Options prices are much more transparent today, especially the options on ETFs. It is much easier to manipulate stocks and sometimes their options, but others like the ETFs options are so big that manipulating them on the U.S. exchanges is quite an arduous task. The awesome thing about options is that there is always a very good quoted price available at any point during the market hours, making it very accessible and liquid.

Chapter Seven:
ETFs Options

The diversity that an exchange traded funds (ETFs) offers is tremendous, you can have access to and profit from the movement of various stocks in the same industry that constitute an ETF. However, with the power of the leverage offered through ETFs options, trading ETFs becomes 'steroid-powered'. As 30th September 2012 investors have embraced ETFs and the total industry assets was approximately $1.3 trillion after 34% year-on-year growth [28].

In fact, some traders have done much of their option trades on ETFs rather than on indices or stocks. I must tell you there are periods in the market when utilising the power of ETFs and especially ETFs options could be the best way forward. These are wonderful at the extremely points in the markets, whether you are bullish or bearish.

Some of the reasons are discussed in this chapter. Now let us do a quick review on the ETFs. What are they and how do they function?

What are ETFs?

An ETF is composed of various individual stocks, and purchased to make up different percentages of the particular ETFs. In essence, when a large institution like a large brokerage, for example, Merrill Lynch, Vanguard, Barclays or State Street, want to create an ETF, they buy shares in various companies and hold them in a trust. A ETFs is very similar to an index or mutual funds but they are different in their creation and how they are traded.

ETFs can be similar to mutual funds in that they sometimes represent a bundle of stocks in a given index or asset class. ETFs do not attract a high fee compared to mutual funds. Unlike mutual funds, they are traded on the stock exchange like common stocks, and also they are more liquid than the mutual funds. They are not subject to hefty and subtle capital gains tax.

Like I said before the nice thing about ETFs is that like stocks and market indices they are optionable! The ETF options are traded like the 'American-style' options, they can be assigned at any time and they expire on the third Friday of the month.

The creations of ETFs and their content stocks is discussed in more details in books dedicated to details on ETFs. I want to show you their importance and how to profit from them.

The Advantages of ETFs Options

First of all, ETFs options are one of the most diverse financial instruments recently created in the stock market lately. Like I said before it is a hybrid of mutual funds and stocks. The most important thing to note is that they are very liquid, you can easily buy and sell them on the market. There is always someone ready to buy at the other end because they are traded in large volumes, therefore the buy and sell spreads are always very narrow, which is a traders dream.

Most especially the ETFs that trail broad market indices are known to trade in higher volumes. As a result they are very' optionable' and offer opportunities for profit. In fact, some ETFs trade in volumes that are higher than most stocks. Since a lot of ETFs are trading in large volumes, this eventually translates to large open interest on their respective options, making their options highly liquid as well. Therefore they have a really tight bid/ask spreads and traders get good fills.

Secondly, because ETFs are a mix of stocks usually in the same industry or sectors, they tend to move together and fall together. What this means is that if one of the components stocks of the ETF is falling they others that are trending up or stable would reduce the risk by averaging out, which would have been much greater had it been that a trader was fully invested in the share of that individual falling stock. ETFs therefore do not produce too much surprise moves, they tend to trend for a much longer period and offer a relaxed atmosphere for trade, by reducing the market 'noise' on an individual stock. While stocks may have more volatile moves- (up and down) moves, there are less surprises with the indices and ETFs.

Thirdly, another favourite thing about the ETFs as discussed earlier is that they are 'optionable'. Not only are they 'optionable', their options are very cheap, they traded in $1 wide strike increments usually, and this is regardless of the price of the underlying ETFs. With this it is always easy for you to find the particular ETFs options strike price that you want, unlike he strike prices of stock options, which could be in $2.5, $5 or more increments.

Fourth, ETFs differ from the mutual funds in the way the prices are calculated. Essentially, mutual funds do not trade during normal market hours. The brokers for the mutual funds take in buy and sell orders from investors during market trading hours, and compute the price of the mutual funds at the end of the day. Therefore for mutual funds the transactions actually occur at the close of the market. If you have ever traded a mutual fund(s), you would notice the price of you funds is only determined at the end of the trading day, unlike ETFs that are constantly traded during the market hours and just like ordinary shares or stocks their prices or value is updated instantaneously all day long.

Table of Indices and their respective ETFs

INDEX	ETFs (CREATORS)
Russell 2000	IWM (ishares)
S&p 500	SPY (SPDRs)
Dow Jones Industrial Average	DIA (SPDRs)
Nasdaq 100 Composite	QQQ (Power Shares)

Even if I wanted to gain exposure to stocks in a country I could buy the ETFs or simply trade the ETF options, for example like EEM, EWZ, etc. If I wanted to gain exposure to the financial sector in the United States, I would get in to the XLF which represents stocks in the financial sector or the XHB for the Home builders. The same goes for the commodities like gold, silver and even oil, so on and so forth. For gold, silver, oil or steel; that would be GLD (SPDR), SLV (iShares) or USO or X respectively, for example. So with the avalanche of new ETFs created and disappearing everyday it is not difficult find the specific one to fit in to my investment objectives. You only need to ensure whatever ETFs you choose to trade, that they are very liquid, have options available on them and that they are backed by reputable firms.

Disadvantages of Trading ETFs

If you think trading ETFs does not have any risks then you are not living in this world. Like any investment vehicle there are risks associated. The most important thing here is that you know what the risks are, which ones are risky, he risk, how to avoid trading them and how to ensure your risks on the good ones you identified to be fitting for you are kept to a minimum; if you do these things you would be here for a long time.

Like any financial instrument, i.e. mutual fund, index or even a stock they fall usually when there is a market downturn and rise as well when there is a rebound. So whenever you trade ETFs remember it is like any other financial instrument it can fall in value. This is similar to what you could get on the value of the ETF options.

Traders must be aware of leveraged ETFs. First of all, leveraged ETFs are a 'double- whammy'. They are ETFs – 'a bundle of stock', so there is already some sort of leverage built in t it, then they have an 'icing on the cake'-they are leveraged. So the way they respond is unpredictable in comparison to movements in the prices of an underlying ETF.

To be honest with you, I would advise you to steer clear of leverage ETFs till you are well experienced in trading ETFs and their options. To improve your ability to profit from ETFs and the leveraged ETFs the best thing is to read the published prospectuses of the respective ETFs and for the first 6 months of your market activity to follow the ETFs you are interested in daily and get used to the pattern and the way the prices fluctuate. The broad-based ETFs for example the SPY and DIA, and those not broad-based for example the XLF (SPDR), which is made up of 84 companies in the banking and financial services area are one of my most preferred.

Criteria for finding an ETF to Trade

Later we would get to our famous beta options strategies, and I would discuss some of the stocks that we have traded options on over the last three years and they have generated thousands of dollars in profits, for example, GMCR. I can send you a list of them if you send me an email with your request to *support@hiqtraders.com*.

In a similar vein, I would discuss some ETFs later in this chapter which you must get yourself familiar with if you want to trade ETFs and or ETFs options. These are the ETFs we trade and we trade them over and over again, regardless of the direction they are moving. First of all, you might be asking how we select these ETFs that make good option trading opportunities. This is what this section is about.

Criteria #1:

Search and Research – Start your search of the best ETFs you want to trade on the markets. Look for the most liquid ETFs available. You can also use google search, your brokerage platforms and other available sources. I have listed some of the most liquid ETFs in the appendix of this book.

Criteria #2:

Group your ETFs - Every ETFs move in tandem sometimes mush faster than the overall broad market index sometimes at a slower pace. Whenever you trade ETFs look at the movement or response of other similar ETFs monitoring the same sector, see their response to the overall market index. This can guide you in to expected moves on the ETFs, whether you expect a stronger or weaker move.

Criteria #3:

Liquidity- as I have always described in this book, liquidity is the juice of any market, without liquidity the prices and trades on an underlying commodity are skewed. ETFs are very liquid, they are very much cheaper options compared to the stock options hence my attraction to them. Their spreads are very narrow, and they can be very volatile and sometimes very predictable.

Drop any illiquid ETFs you have in your collections and always ensure you keep refining them regularly to ensure you have the best selection, in terms of volume and costs, all the time. Avoid any ETFs with volume of less than 1.2 million traded shares per day.

Criteria #4:

Learning Curve- the commonest ETFs are more liquid, but remember they are other opportunities out there seek them. The QQQ, SPY, DIA, GLD, EWJ, FXI are one of the most heavy traded ones, there are lots more by the way. So start with those ones you are familiar with. Watch them for a week, save their daily chart in a folder, look at the daily movements on them, their response to movements in the overall index. After about 3 weeks of study you should be able to build on your knowledge and start trading some little volumes/ contracts on them, and learn, that is the true way to be a trader.

Criteria #5:

Apart from the liquidity on the particular option contract on the ETF you want to trade, ensure it has sufficient open interest. Do not trade option contract that are too far from the money, they sometimes do not respond to the move in the underlying ETFs quickly as you would expect. If you not too sure then do not trade strike prices more $5 away from the current price of the particular ETF.

However, having said that I have seen some tremendous opportunities in trading some option contracts that are out-of –the-money that were cheap to enter therefore providing a lucrative trade opportunity.

In a previous chapter I eliminated ETFs where the front month option open interest is low – by saying too low, I meant that the open interest should be large enough that any time your order makes up only a small percentage of the orders fed in to the exchange, in reality open interest in an option do not matter to your probability of making a profit.

Finally, for a list of websites on ETFs go to Appendix 3.

The Most Liquid ETFs on the Markets which you know:

I already discussed what we look for in ETFs before we buy and sell options on them in the previous section. I would now do a brief discussion on each of the ETFs that fulfill our criteria.

Since the advent of ETFs on the stock market, they have become a tool for investors to trade different financial assets and produce some outstanding profits in the markets. ETFs have become a transparent and a very cost-effective way to trade market volatility providing access to different markets in different regions of the world and in to very wide range of sectors, commodities, countries, indexes, currencies and assets; while investors enjoy the security from the very fact that they are regulated by exchanges in the United States.

Options on ETFs have provided some extra boost to the power of ETFs, providing easier and more attractive ways to speculate and control risk. That is, buying calls and puts limits the buyer's risk to the cost of a contract, which is always a smaller fraction of the cost of buying/shorting the actual ETF, but these calls/puts still lets the buyer profit from favorable moves thereby exaggerating the profits in proportion to the total cost of the options.

Let us get to business and discuss each of the most liquid ETFs briefly;

1. SPDR S&P 500; SPY (Ticker symbol SPY; primary benchmark is S&P 500)

SPDR S&P 500 SPY is one the most liquid and actively traded ETFs on the stock exchange, it was created January 1993[22]. It has an average volume of over 85 million shares as at time of writing[22], and options on it has a very large open interest. Its benchmark is the S&P 500, and it moves very closely with its price.

2. SPDR Gold Trust; GLD

SPDR® Gold Shares (GLD) was created November 2004 and traded on the NYSE Arca since December 13, 2007 to closely mimic the movement in the value of gold in U.S. Dollars, offering traders, speculators and investors the opportunity to trade gold in various creative ways which are relatively cost efficient and secure, for examples buying and selling options on them. SPDR® Gold Shares is one of the largest physically backed gold exchange traded fund (ETF) in the world. It has over 28,364,468 ounces of physical gold to back its prices and as a trust it is valued at over to $37.35 billion[27]. Recently John Paulson who famously made over $15 billion in the recent subprime mortgage crisis in 2007[2], made a $736 million loss in the second quarter of 2013[8] on this ETFs. The SPDR® Gold Shares is also traded on the Singapore Stock Exchange, Tokyo Stock Exchange, The Stock Exchange of Hong Kong and the Mexican Stock Exchange (BMV)[27]. It trades over nine million in daily average volume.

3. iShares MSCI Brazil Capped Index; EWZ

The ishares MSCI Brazil Capped ETF gives investors exposure to the Brazilian large- and mid-cap stocks. This ETF has an average volume of over 10 million per day[29] and with very liquid options as well. It has become one of the proven ways for investors in the United States to get access to opportunities in the booming Brazilian economy.

4. iShares FTSE/Xinhua China 25 Index; FXI

The FXI tracks the prices of the 25 largest and most liquid stocks in China. All the stocks on this list are traded on the Hong Kong Stock Exchange and they are all constituents of the FTSE All-World Index.[12]

Some of the stocks listed on the FXI are China Mobile Ltd, China Construction Bank, China Life Insurance,

Agricultural Bank of China, Bank of China, Tencent Holdings Ltd, Ind. & Comm. Bank of China, China Petroleum and Chemicals, PetroChina Co. Ltd, China Overseas Land and Invest., China Shenhua Energy, China Telecom Corp., China Unicom Hong Kong Ltd, Belle International Holdings, China Pacific Insurance, and so on and so forth. In terms of sector distribution, they are financials (55%), telecoms (16%), oil and gas (12%), technology (7%), basic materials (3.8%), consumer goods (3.1%) and industrials and securities (1% approx.)[12].

5. Barclays 20 Year Treasury Bond Fund; TLT

TLT tracks the index of U.S. treasury bonds with maturation in the excess of 20 years, that are non-convertible and obviously dominated in U.S. dollars[11]. Most of the bonds held have maturity of over 25 years (approx. 96%) and just over 3% would mature between 20-25 years [11]. State and local government bonds and targeted investors notes are excluded from this index.

6. Silver Trust; SLV

The most well-known silver ETFs o the market today, with net asset value of over $7.41 billion dollars, back by physical silver. The prices are set via the London Silver Fix Price, which is the price of silver per ounce as determined the three market marking member of the London Bullion Markets Association at 12pm Noon London time every trading day [14].

7. PowerShares; QQQ

The QQQ is the symbol of this ETF and it is hosted by Invesco Invesco PowerShares Capital Management LLC. PowerShares Capital Management LLC is one of the very good providers of highest quality investment management in the world[9].

PowerShares QQQ™, formerly known as "QQQ" or the "NASDAQ-100 Index Tracking Stock®", is an exchange-traded fund based on the Nasdaq-100 Index®. Under normal circumstances, the fund consists of all of stocks in the Nasdaq-100 Index®[19].

The Nasdaq-100 Index® includes 100 of the largest domestic and international nonfinancial companies listed on the Nasdaq Stock Market based on market capitalization. The Fund and the Index are rebalanced quarterly and reconstituted annually [9, 19]. Popular stocks in this index which the QQQ mirrors are Apple, Microsoft, Google, Amazon, Qualcomm, Intel Corp., Gilead Sciences, Cisco Systems, Comcast Corp. and Amgen are among the top holding in the ETF[9, 19].

8. Market Vectors TR Gold Miners; GDX

Market Vectors Gold Miners ETF is an exchange-traded fund incorporated in the USA, which seeks to mirror the price of the Arca Gold Miners Index[1]. Top holdings include GoldCorp Inc., Barrick Gold Corp., Newmont Mining Corp.,

Randgold Resources Ltd, Yamana gold Inc., Franco-Nevada Corp., Silver Wheaton Corp., Kinross Gold Corp., AngloGold Ashanti Ltd and Agnico Eagle Mines Ltd[1].

9. *iPath S&P 500 VIX Short-Term Futures ETN; VXX*

VXX is managed by Barclays Funds with a total market cap of 1.19 billion dollars[30]. The fund is linked to the performance of the S&P 500 VIX Short-Term Futures Index. This index, that is, S&P 500 VIX Short-Term Futures Index, accesses the equity market volatility through CBOE Volatility Index futures[17]. The index is held in futures contract so that it can be rolled on a month-to-month basis[17].

10. *iShares MSCI Emerging Markets Index; EEM*

iShares MSCI Emerging Markets Index is owned by BlackRock. Total asset holdings within the EEM includes Samsung Electronics, Taiwan Semiconductor, China Mobile, Tencent Holdings, Chain Construction Bank, Gazprom, America Movil SAB, Ind & Comm Bank of China and Hyundia Motor, Naspers Ltd[13]. Total net asset as of Dec., 2nd 2013 was $42.2 billion dollars[13].

11. *Financial Select Sector SPDR; XLF*

Total net asset value is 15.35 billion dollars[16]. Some of top holdings includes: Berkshire Hathaway Inc., Wells Fargo & Co., JPMorgan Chase, Bank of America, Citigroup, American

International Group, American Express Co., U.S. Bancorp, The Goldman Sachs Group Inc. and MetLife Inc.[21]

12. Daily Small Cap Bear 3X Shares; TZA

Direxion Daily Small Cap Bear 3X Shares is one of the most liquid ETFs that I have so much interest in, it is a leveraged ETF, with daily volumes in excess of 12 million shares or more, with several thousands of calls and puts available for different strike prices. The fund seeks results by giving investors the opportunity to profit from three times the fall in value of the Russell 2000® Index (300%).

The Russell 2000® Index measures the performance of the small-cap segment of the U.S. equity universe and is comprised of the smallest 2000 companies in the Russell 3000® Index[7]. The stocks in the Russell 2000® Index presents approximately 10% of the total market capitalization of Russell 2000®[7].

13. Energy Select Sector SPDR; XLE

Top holdings in this index includes[23]; Exxon Mobil Corp., Chevron Corp., Slumberger, Occidental Petroleum Corp., ConocoPhillips, Pioneer Natural Resources, EOG Resources Inc., Halliburton Company, Anadarko Petroleum Corp., and National Olwell Varco Inc. among others.

Putting all together so far, ETFs options a numerous these days and they have become very liquid. Lots of big pension funds, hedge funds and individual traders from all over the world are trading them now. The best markets to trade are the liquid ones which guarantee your order fills during market trading hours and you can easily trade them to lock in your profits. ETFs gives you that power easily. The strike prices of ETFs are always very close to the current market price of the underlying ETFs offering reasonable short-term profits.

Chapter Eight: Leverage ETFs and Options: How to trade them

Leveraged ETFs is very similar to ETFs the only difference is that they are structured to respond to movement in the underlying index in multiple of two or three. That is, if the underlying moves by 1 point a double-leveraged ETF would move twice in response to the price. It does provide new opportunities to active traders on a daily basis, but I would discuss the intricacies in this chapter and some tips on trading them and the options on them.

Leveraged ETFs are available for most of the well-known indexes, such as the Dow Jones Industrial Average and the S&P 500 including the Nasdaq 100. One thing that is very central to trading leveraged ETFs and their options is that they do not amplify the annual returns of an index rather it tracks the daily changes in the price of its underlying index.

A leveraged fund with a 3:1 ratio would add extra $2 borrowed funds for every $1 invested. If the underlying index moves by 1% today then the fund would move by 3%. The broker would deduct fees, including management fees and transaction costs. The reverse would be the case for inverse leveraged ETFs. A drop in 1% would lead to a drop in 3% for this same fund. Funds like these keep a constant amount of leverage, for example 2:1 or 3:1 ratio during the fund's lifespan. This leverage is produced through swap agreements and futures contracts on the underlying index

Most leveraged ETFs and inverse ETFs are meant to track the *daily changes in the price* of its underlying index thereby offering investors profit from the indexes they track. Performances of the leveraged ETFs over a day timeframe is highly unpredictable, they are not designed to deliver long term returns. Leveraged ETFs clearly from their names are leveraged, some of them have lost over 90-95% of their value since their inception, so they can be very volatile and risky.

Another important distinction here is the mutual funds, the ETFs are very similar to mutual funds, and however they are some differences and advantages that ETFs have over the mutual funds. ETFs trade the exact stocks that are traded on an index, therefore they can be bought and sold the same day. Mutual funds can only be traded at the end of the trading day that is when their prices are recalculated and rebalanced and the net asset value determined. If you bought a mutual funds yesterday and you check the price today when the market is open you would not be quoted the price till the end of the trading day.

The cost of ETFs is lower compared to mutual funds, as there are managing costs charged by the portfolio managers which is not the case for ETFs, except for brokerage trading costs.

Traditional broad based ETFs offer fairly close performance to the daily movement of the underlying index, unlike the leveraged and or the inverse ETFs they do anything other than track the daily movement in the index price. Leveraged ETFs are strictly for those who trade daily, in fact they carry higher costs compared to average broad based ETFs. Some have expense ratios of about 0.85% compared to 0.25%.

The most important things to know about leveraged ETFs are:

Trading leveraged ETF can result in more than expected losses, as they are magnified compared to the losses seen when the target ETF decrease in the value. One important thing about trading leverage is to determine which direction you anticipate the market to move and once you achieve this target or not you are out of the market, that is, you close the trade. For this strategy, you day trade only. For example, when you strongly bullish, you buy a leveraged ETFs that moves up when the index or ETF you are tracking moves up, that is, because if you are right the gains would be magnified and if you are wrong, they would be magnified as well.

Also since we are clear on the fact that leveraged ETFs rebalance daily, they aren't designed to be held overnight. The daily rebalancing is called "beta slippage". All the price movements of leveraged ETFs are calculated daily on a percentage basis for that day and that day only, and the same process starts all over the next trading day. However, if you trade intra-day constantly, apart from the cots it may lead to your trading account being placed on some restrictions depending on your brokers' rules, classifying you as a 'pattern day trader'.

Some of the most popular leveraged ETFs are:

ETF	TOTAL ASSETS	AVERAGE DAILY VOLUME	EXPENSE RATIO	LEVERAGE FACTOR	INDEX / UNDERLYING
TNA	$618.41 MILLION	10.97 MILLION	0.95%	3X	RUSSELL 2000 INDEX
SSO	$1.57 BILLION	7.07 MILLION	0.92%	2X	S&P 500 INDEX
FAS	$1.13 BILLION	5.97 MILLION	0.95%	3X	RUSSELL 1000 FINANCIAL SERVICES INDEX
QLD	$608.19 MILLION	3.72 MILLION	0.95%	2X	NASDAQ 100 INDEX
UPRO	$311.91 MILLION	2.32 MILLION	0.95%	3X	S&P 500 INDEX
ERX	$255.05 MILLION	1.55 MILLION	0.95%	3X	ENERGY SELECT SECTOR INDEX
UWM	$693.30 MILLION	1.55 MILLION	0.98%	2X	RUSSELL 2000 INDEX
AGQ	$980.26 MILLION	1.48 MILLION	0.95%	2X	SILVER BULLION
DDM	$215.82 MILLION	518,000	0.95%	2X	DOW JONES INDUSTRIAL AVERAGE INDEX
UST	$19.81 MILLION	476,000	0.95%	2X	BARCLAYS CAPITAL U.S 7-10 YEAR TREASURY INDEX

Guide to the 10 Most Popular Leveraged ETFs [28]

Let us describe this here, let us say I paid $500 for one share of a particular 3x leveraged ETF based on an index that's currently at 20,000. That same day, the index goes up 20%

and closes at 24,000. As a result, your share will increase 60% to $800. This is what we love as traders, but you should always look at the other side as well, remember there are two sides to a coin. If a trader decides to carry that trade to the next trading day, and the index now falls from 24,000 to 20,000 back to where it started from that would be a 16.66% drop. Now our 3x leveraged ETFs would fall 49.99% for that next trading day.

To the naked eye is it not a bad trade, since the day before it was up 60% and today it dropped 49.99%, but 49.99% of $800 is $400. Therefore my share would be worth $400. So instead of having a $300 profit I have a $100 loss. So despite the fact that the index was back to where it started from my share price is 20% down from the start at $400. This is effect of multiple trading days on leveraged ETFs. See what I mean! One thing to bear in mind is that though I would not encourage you get too much involved in day trading, trading on a daily basis can lead to more transaction costs. If at any time you decide to keep your leveraged ETFs positions for more than a day, then I would personally suggest that you keep an eye on the underlying index and what could move the market in favour or against your opened positions.

Secondly, leveraged ETFs are already a 'designer' trading tool, that is, they have been 'leveraged'. Now if you want to trade them as an option, you must be very careful, or at least have a plan in mind at the onset and do not get creative with things, like doing a spread or whatever on them.

The reason being that if you decide to use these complicated ETFs for any trading purpose other than the primary intent can become a monster difficult to manage let alone control its risks. If you desire to trade options on ETFs then trade them on the ETFs, don't be tempted to trade options on leveraged ETFs.

Thirdly, as I described earlier one must be mindful of the brokerage costs and fees when trading leveraged ETFs daily. Therefore before you enter a leverage ETFs trade one must decide the exit when if gains or if losses ensues and consider leverage ETFs to be skewed by design. Have a clear goal, and don't get greedy once you've met it. There is only a very short time to turn profit, cover the costs and fees and any possible taxes on gains.

Fourth, once the trade does not go in your favour be ready to abandon the leveraged ETF trade, in spite of little losses, be ready to jump off the ship. If in time it turns around and goes north, forget about it, don't go back and forth checking on the price and don't not exaggerate the pain.

Fifth, always have keep your mind on the breaking news throughout the trading day, and after the market closes as well. Also ensure you are on the board for upcoming news and announcements like the Fed, the European Central Bank reports, etc. The market is never rational and does not always discount news. The market could stay irrational for long before your trades become profitable.

Sixth, since I have tried to convince you that getting in and out of the leveraged ETFs trade in most cases within a day is essential to success, I would advise that you stick with the more liquid ones. As such you would be able to get in and out quickly, and be able to find a buyer readily, ensuring you get narrow spreads on your bid-ask. Bear in mind that any security no matter how liquid do go through periods of increased price fluctuations which may cause them to have gaps in price. As a general rule, if and whenever I want to trade leveraged ETFs, I trade the ones with at least an average daily volume of at least two to two and half million shares.

When trying to get out of a leveraged ETFs ensure you get out early before the end of the day, because due to the fact that other traders are trying to get out as well, it may cause the orders to be skewed affecting the normal narrow spread between the bid and the ask. Getting out at least 30 minutes before the closing bell is ideal.

Lastly, never let go of your mind and never allow the market to be out of your sight when you have a leveraged ETF trade open, more so if you have an option on it opened. Ensure you have ready access to the internet at home and away whenever you are in such trades.

Chapter Nine:
ETFs vs. Index Options

Starting this chapter I would use the market indices as examples. The S&P 500 Index tracks the overall market performance of the large-cap stocks in the United States, the Dow Jones Industrial Average tracks the 30 largest U.S. companies and the Russell 2000 Index tracks the performance of 2,000 small-cap stocks in the United States and the stock market 'fear' index is tracked by the VIX®.

Therefore, a market "index" is simply a measure that tracks the overall performance of market sector(s) or a given combination of financial asset. This chapter is written to clearly discuss how you can trade these indexes and the difference between them. It was very difficult to trade indexes in years gone, but with the versatility of options trading today, this has been much easier to do.

Now different families of funds have their own tracker, or index for tracking the performance of a particular index, and there are options available for trading them if there are liquid enough. For example, the State Street Global Advisors offers a tracker for the S&P 500 index called the SPY (S&P500 SPDRs: NYSE) which trades over 110 million in share volume daily (an average of 90 days trading days) [18]. This SPY is an ETF. In the same way the Vanguard family of funds also offers a variety of index funds which includes Vanguard S&P 500 Index Fund, it also tracks the S&P 500. This is the VOO (Vanguard S&P500 ETFs : NYSE) with an average volume of 3 million daily [31], suffice to say, that the SPY closely mimics the movement on the S&P than the VOO, therefore it is more liquid and has more liquid options.

Another example here is Gold. You can trade gold as a commodity on the futures exchanges, the COMEX and CBOT, and also as an ETFs SPDR Gold Trust Shares (GLD: NYSE).

I have listed some ETFs with their tickers and on the other side of the table itemised the indices they track. There are other similar funds that have created other ETFs to track the S&P for example, but like I explained above but they might not be as popular. VOO is also a very popular fund, and it is also closely reflects the movements in the S&P than other funds in the market.

TICKER	INDEX TRACKED
DJX	DOW JONES INDUSTRIAL AVERAGE INDEX OPTIONS
SPX	S&P 500 INDEX OPTIONS
VIX	CBOE VOLATILITY INDEX® (VIX®) OPTIONS
RUT	RUSSELL 2000 INDEX
NDX	NASDAQ 100 INDEX OPTIONS
OEX	S&P 100 INDEX OPTIONS (AMERICAN STYLE)
RUI	RUSSELL 1000 INDEX

There really no trading per se going on in the individual index itself. The tracking ETFs offers trading opportunity to trade these indexes in ways never available before. The options on them allows one to make money or hedge profits on the price movements of the underlying index.

ETFs and ETF Options

I have been talking about ETFs for now, but ETF as I described in an earlier chapter is actually a mutual fund that trades like a stock, and therefore options could be traded on it. At any time during the day traders could buy and sell an ETF and its options just like a stock, and benefit from a broad-based movement in the overall constituents of the ETFs itself unlike buying and selling individual stocks. Most of the available EFTs trade a basket of similar stocks in the same industry, like housing, consumer products, etc., and they trade with very low costs; unlike mutual funds which can only be bought and sold at the end of the day when their net asset value is rebalanced.

The advent of ETFs have made opportunities for trading the following financial asset available. Just think of any market, sectors, market niche, foreign market niche or anything tradable there is an ETF for it. Traders can now take long and/or short positions and even leveraged positions on them. These includes;

- Domestic and Foreign Stock Indexes (large-cap, small-cap, growth, value, sector, etc.)
- Currencies (yen, euro, pound, dollar, Canadian dollars, Australian dollars, etc.)
- Commodities (physical commodities like gold, silver, platinum, financial assets, commodity indexes, etc.)
- Bonds (treasury, corporate, municipal bonds and international bonds)

The Most Liquid ETFs with high Trading Volume on their Options:

EFT	TICKER
SPDR TRUST	SPY
POWERSHARES QQQ TRUSTS	QQQQ
FINANCIAL SELECT SECTOR SPDR	XLF
ISHARES RUSSELL 2000 INDEX FUND	IWM
ISHARES FTSA/XINHUA CHINA 25	FXI
ISHARES MSCI EMERGING MARKETS INDEX	EEM
SPDR ENERGY SECTOR	XLE
ISHARES MSCI BRAZIL INDEX FUND	EWZ
US NATURAL GAS FUND ETF	UNG
ISHARES SILVER TRUST	SLV
SPDR GOLD TRUST	GLD
MARKET VECTORS GOLD MINERS	GDX
SPDR S&P RETAIL	XRT
ISHARES MSCI EAFE INDEX FUND	EFA
SPDR DOW JONES INDUSTRIAL AVERAGE ETF	DIA

A lot of ETFs come and go, depending on their appeal to the trading public, it is a survival of the fittest. If an ETF or a mutual fund does not have enough publicity and volume they tend to close down, in fact now and again, here and there you would see new funds popping up and disappearing based on their structure, appeal and subscriber base. That is why you would see adverts on the TV and smartphones today on new funds to appeal to traders and investors alike.

It is important to ensure that the ETF you want to trade tracks its underlying index very closely and that it is very liquid, to ensure that you can get in and out at you bidding easily.

Whatever you want to buy or sell in the market today there would be an ETF for it. For example, if you are considering going long or short on real estate there is a fund or ETF for it and so on and so forth. In fact some ETFs are structured to go short only on the real estate market, some are just for the bulls and some are just structured to track the ETF or index very closely.

As discussed already ETFs are optionable, and in fact unlike the stock options they are cheaper in price (I mean you could literarily buy one contract for $0.15 cents and re-sell it in 48 hours for $0.65), more liquid and less susceptible to manipulation by floor traders because of the low implied volatility, and their movements are somewhat very predictable. In reality if a ETFs bid/ask spread is wide, about $0.05-$0.1 spread review you intentions to buy it properly, you need to check the average daily volume and the open interest.

MAKE MONEY CONSISTENTLY TRADING OPTIONS

For example, above you see the chart of the DIA, an ETF which tracks the Dow jones Industrial average very closely. Currently on the chart the ETF is trading somewhere close to $154.77, and the chart below is of the DIA Dec 13 158 call option and it was priced at just slightly over $1 about seven trading days prior.

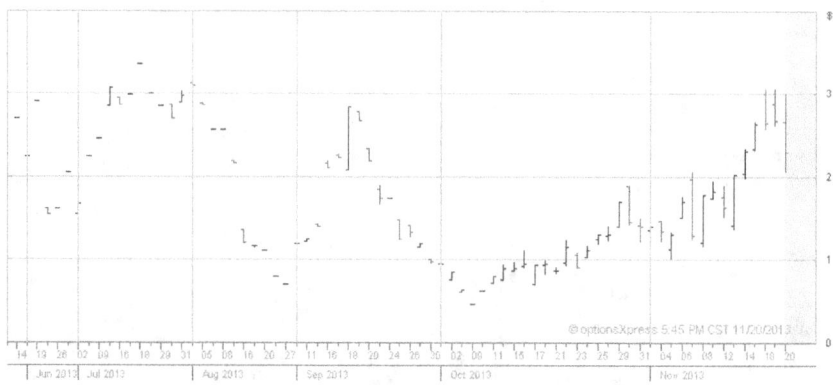

Chart of DIA Dec 13 158 call, Courtesy of OptionsXpress.com®

The chart of another very liquid ETFs below, the FXI (iShares FTSE China 25 Index Fund; NYSE), this ETF was trading at about $39.57 on the 20th November 2013, however if you look at the other chart below it the options shows a different price story.

MAKE MONEY CONSISTENTLY TRADING OPTIONS

The FXI Dec 2013 39.5 call options was priced at about $1.2 on the 4th of November and it rose to just under $3 on the 19th November. Omg! You see what I mean!

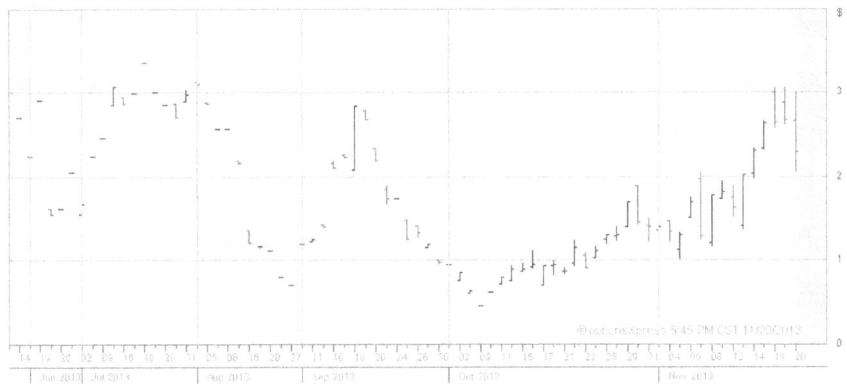

Chart of FXI Dec 13 39.5 call, Courtesy of OptionsXpress.com®

Remember, just for recap, ETFs are structured investment vehicle and they are a bunch of stocks in a related industry or a sector or an index. They are like mutual funds, but they traded like stocks. Anything you just feel like trading, trust me you can find an ETF for it, whether it is in consumer stocks, commodities, agricultural stocks, real estate/home builders, etc. you would find an ETF for it.

And since most sectors move up in tandem, ETFs could be wonderful. For example, when I want to buy an options on REGN and it is very highly priced I tend to look at BIIB or QCOR and see if the options there are affordable. Since I am anticipating a northward move on REGN I could expect the share prices of BIIB or QCOR to also move upwards as well. So other options of another similar share that are priced lower could be a way out. In such a case when an ETF is available you simple buy the ETF or ETFs on pharmaceutical, period.

So simply as we all know that a positive move on the REGN would trigger a similar move on the similar shares (i.e. especially in the same sector) I would expect the ETFs on that industry (and their options which are much cheaper) to move up as well. Hence, I would not miss out on the price move and profits should in case I am not sure of the stock to buy in that particular industry.

Before I itemise some of the differences between the index and stock options, I would described the way stock and index options are exercised and the A.M. /P.M. settlements for the options.

American- or European-style exercise.

We have described in chapter one and two that stock options are exercised the American-style exercise, which means they can be exercised or assigned any time before the options expire, at any time before their expiration date.

Unlike index options which could have either American or European-style options exercise. That is their options can only be exercised or assigned on the last day of the expiration of the options.

Apparently, if you are selling options, calls or puts, you would prefer the European-style options as there is no risk of early assignment.

The AM/PM settlement

Settlement basically means how the final price of the underlying whether stock options or index options are calculated therefore influencing how much they are exchanged for. Typically, stock options expires on the third Saturday of the month, but as we know that there is no trading on Saturday the day they are settled, the price for their settlement is at the close of third Friday of the month. Therefore, they have a PM settlement.

Most index options have PM settlement, some do have AM settlement. What this means is that their prices are calculated with the opening prices on the next trading day following their expiration date. In this case, Thursday is the last trading day before expiration, and the final settlement prices of these index options would be valued on their price when the market opens on Friday. Clearly, this means that if you were in price or if the price for your traded options closed at a high price on Thursday it could gap up or down at the open on Friday. This could a good or devastating impact on your profits.

Difference between ETF options and Index Options

There are several important differences between index options and options on ETFs. The most significant of these revolves around the fact that trading options on ETFs can result in the need to assume or deliver shares of the underlying ETF (this may or may not be viewed as a benefit by some). This is not the case with index options.

Most index options as described above are 'European-styled' in the way they are exercised. They settle in cash. They can be bought or sold at any point in time prior to expiration, but they can only be exercised on expiration. Unlike index options, the options on stocks are 'American-style' that is they settle with exchange of the stocks of the shares, therefore they could be exercised at any point in time prior to their expiation.

Chapter Ten:
Beta Options Strategies

This book was written to enable you to equip yourself with the basic knowledge to make money consistently from the market without the usual complexity of options. It is intended to make trading options simple. This is the reason for the earlier chapters, they were written for you to understand the basics of option trading. This chapter is for you to learn how to 'star-gaze' in to the options market pick out stocks to pounce on that are ready to bounce in price and volume. Most importantly, you would learn how to spot simple and consistent patterns on charts that are obvious, and that are guaranteed to produce profits, where up or down in most market conditions.

In this chapter I would go through some charts and I would show you how I spot the obvious trend from charts and how I enter in to out-of-the-money options (OTM). I enter them to benefit from maximum price spike that is about to happen. This chapter is written most especially for high beta options, however once you get the trick, I can send you a list of stocks to watch that I update every 2-3 weeks for movement, and you can watch these stock for these patterns to occur. Another way I use this method is that once I find a very predictable price movement on a particular stock I tend to buy in and sell out on the stocks in-the-money options and profit from them regularly, sometimes over the span of 6 months. One very good example is the GMCR that stock was a cash-cow for most of 2012-2013 for calls options, I had a 40-2 wins on all my options contracts on that stock alone and even milking it on its way down in the Fall of 2013 with puts!

Without further ado let us get in to the meat of this chapter. Once you get the tips in this chapter you are guaranteed to make at least 50- 125% monthly trading options, and when you do please send me an email to share your testimonials on support@hiqtraders.com.

The information in this chapter should be illegal for all intents and purposes, and no where will you get this information that I am about to share with you for this cheap. You would get the same information sold to you via monthly software subscription to pick the stocks for you by some guy and they charge you over $250 for the monthly subscription, some even sell the book and course and waste your time for 2 hours and finally share only a bit of what I am about to show you at the final 15 minutes of the over-priced presentation just to whet your appetite and charge for an ongoing fee to teach you the rest and some do charge over $2,500 for this same principles.

However, smile, you have all the details here. In life complex things have a simple way for them to be grasped, when you cannot teach a theory to a high school graduate then to me that is not an applicable theory in reality. Once you meet someone that understands a complex thing they would make it look so simple, that is what I am about to show you. Eighty percent of the cost of this book is entirely this chapter, but I have saved the rest for the last. In other words this chapter accounts for 80% of the price of this book.

Like I always say, if you are going to spend $10,000 in investment money would it not make sense to find some experts to give you some advice before you part with your money? Besides research says that only professional hire experts anyway, so paying some few dollars for this book to show you how money is made on Wall Street is not too much.

When you read too many technical signals in to any trade then you are either going to lose money or not going to make money, because most indicators say the same thing or contradict each other, leading to analysis-paralysis. Mind you traders on the floor do not have the time to sieve through tones of data or details before they make a trade, they have the basic charts and indicators that they look at and then base their decisions on them. This is what I am about to show, welcome to trading options on steroids!!!

The principle of this chapter is that "the chart tells it all". With this idea I use our "beta software" to search for stocks that are optionable with high volume ready for a bounce. Over the last 7 years of trading options I have discovered that sometimes these stocks may not be popular stocks, sometimes their options do not necessary have massive volumes, however they behave in the same way, they may be due for an earnings reports, and mostly importantly they have been short-squeezed!

Automatic Beta Options Principles

I have tailored and diluted these facts in to what I called the "Automatic Beta Options Principles".

To put things in to perspective in terms of money, now if you buy 10 options contracts of a particular stock, say for example at $1.4 per contract and the price of the option contract moves to $2.4 automatically you have made $1,000 profit (this could slightly be less after the broker deducts their commission and exchange filing fees, these would usually not be more than $17 per 10 option contracts you trade, depending on your broker).

So if the 10 options contracts you bought went up to $3.4 in value your profit becomes $2,000. For those who do not understand how I arrived at this figure, read this: 10

contracts of this hypothetical stock would cost you $1.4 x 1,000 (10 options contracts, as 1 options contracts represent 100); so $(2.4 -1.4) x 1,000 = $1,000; and $(3.4 -1.4) x 1,000 = $2,000.

So if the trader bought 20 contracts, the profit would be $2,000 for each $1 move of the options contract. That is, $(2.4 -1.4) x 2,000 = $2,000; and $(3.4 -1.4) x 2,000 = $4,000. You see!

Now, the next idea is to keep our cost of premium low enough to be able to make profit from the stock move when it happens, but not too low that it could expire worthless without making the anticipated move. Obviously our choice is the OTM (out-of-the-money) options they are cheap enough and comparatively their move is much higher geometrically compared to other options in the option chain.

Automatic Beta Options Principle #1:

Like I said before, floor traders do not have the time and patience to study charts on the floor, they need to make split seconds decisions and buy or sell stocks and need to show results otherwise they would be fired. They do not have the luxury of reviewing tens of indicators like amateurs traders do, because by the time it takes them to study a chart that way — and identify all of the tons of signals involved in pure technical analysis to make a decision— they would have missed a perfect trading opportunity on making 2 or 3 winning trades. So they use other simple strategies to make their trade decisions.

One of their popular indicators is obvious, identifying of support and resistance points... because all indicators are the same, the fewer the better. When you look at charts usually on the long-term time frames (6-month and 12-month chart), one thing becomes obvious, that the prices bounces off and or retraces to a particular point, like we say in trading everything retraces to the mean.

When stocks are trending upwards they typically find support at these price levels and stocks that are trending down would likely find resistance at these levels. It is then a sufficient and safe proposition that it is safe to buy calls if prices keeps bouncing of these points. And if down-trending stocks are selling off at these levels, it's safe to buy puts.

The following trade on **Joy Global (JOY: NYSE)** is an obvious example, let us see below.

MAKE MONEY CONSISTENTLY TRADING OPTIONS

Clearly, by looking at these chart above you would see that the Joy Global price keeps bouncing off upwards at the $49 mark, so in Early August 2013 we purchased calls and sold off at the time it touched the $53 mark for an outstanding **250% gains on the call options**.

We did something that was a great, again in late August we re-bought the calls again and sold for another **300% gain, in JUST ONE MONTH!!!**

Just by repeating this same technique on every stock we have consistently made huge gains.

Here is another example, CLGX (Corelogic: NYSE) between September 9, 2013 and October 21, 2013 CLGX has been trending between $26 and $28 per share. The RIS above has been bouncing off at that range price and the MACD below were close together, this is a combination of a short-squeeze stock (this is the second principle discussed below) showing resistance at a price, it was a perfect storm.

We bought calls on it on Oct 23 and within 24 hours our calls purchased for less than $0.5 went up to $2.5. See the CLGX Nov13: 30 calls options chart below, it was an amazing profit, 400% to be precise.

So if you invested $2,000 you would have definitely made at least $7,950 after fees and commissions. Not bad for

24hours work, and sure bet there is no other game like this in town!

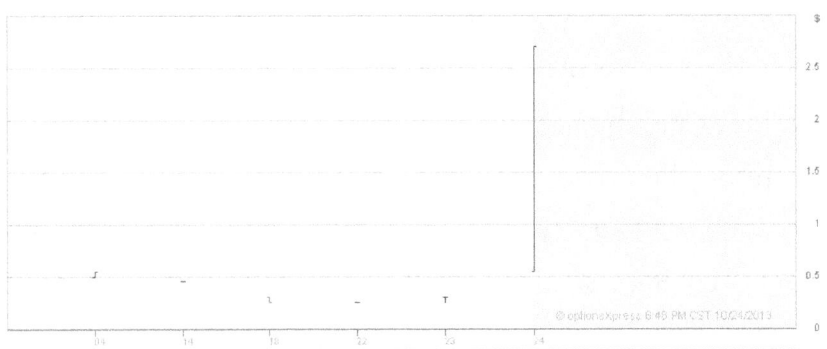

©optionsxpress CLGX Nov13: 30 calls

Automatic Beta Options Principle #2:

Another strategy which have worked repeatedly and has proven itself for me is the "Compressed-Gas Effect" on stocks. It is a way for me to determine short-squeezed stocks. The data on short-squeeze are released about 2 weeks late, and in some cases even with paid service you could get it a week late, that would have given the short-sellers time to cover their shorts and such trades opportunities would have been long gone even before you see it. So my alternative way of determining that is crude but it works almost 80% of the time.

Over the last 5 years I have discovered simple ways to identify over-shorted stocks, and then buy the options on them and the profits on them have been phenomenal. So like I said earlier, the charts tells the story, most of the time. For example, in late July 2013, we found that Facebook was over-shorted in the market by looking at the chart. The stock has been falling in price since it was listed on the markets. Even the employees were selling their stocks fast as soon as they had the opportunity to, it was 'all-rush-for the-exit-door' type of scenario on Facebook shares. So once we saw this happening we were on the prowl, this kind of scenario always leads to a short-squeeze. Even a slightly better than expected results would lead to a massive bounce in price for the stock.

Any way as Facebook slowly came on my radar-watch I kept searching for the right time to enter on some calls. There was so much pessimism about internet companies and social media especially around that time. I can't tell you enough how social media is so important to our lives, there are some things that are here to stay at least for a while and in to the foreseeable future, Facebook is one of them. Now see the chart below,

MAKE MONEY CONSISTENTLY TRADING OPTIONS

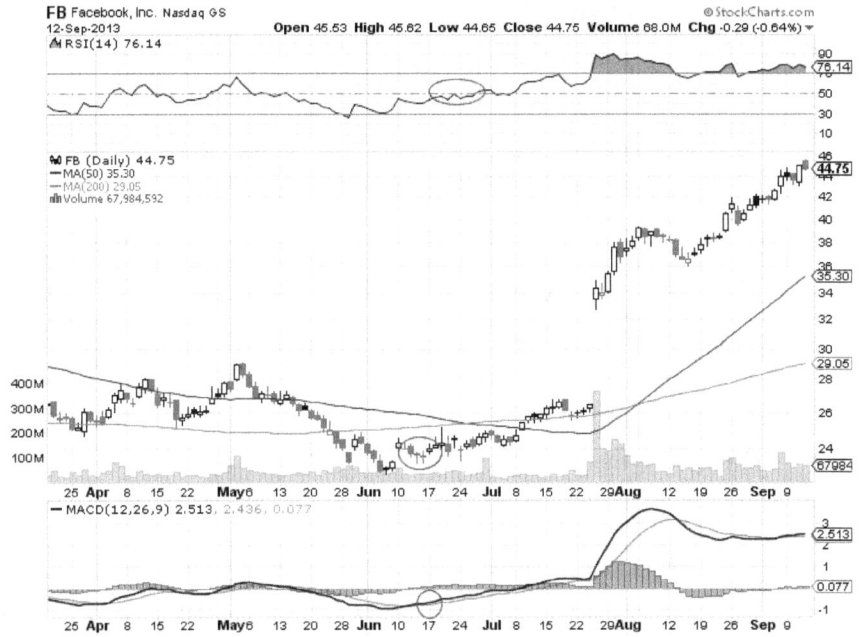

Facebook was at $23-24 a share between June/early July 2013, then slowly it began to rise to about $26 around late July 2013. However, looking at the RSI above it was rising, it was a strong sign that there was accumulation going on the shares of Facebook.

We decided to buy calls on Facebook options, but here is the icing on the cake, because the stock has been shorted too long we could not do a reasonable prediction on the month on which to buy for the calls, so we bought calls that have a bit of expiration in them about 60 days away, and they were cheap, as the puts on Facebook were pricey then, see as calls go up on a particular share the puts would ultimately go down in value.

The rest of the chart tells the story, within five days of purchasing the calls options on Facebook the shares went up to $35 and we saw a tremendous profit on our calls options. We made over **450% profits** from this one trade. Once we saw our signals on Facebook, we knew a pop would happen.

This second principle was also described for the CLGX chart above under the first automatic principle.

Automatic Beta Options Principle #3- the Tsunami-Effect:

Another Secret that I use is the 50 day moving average statistic in combination with the MACD, just like in the first principle when two signals align together like this it is usually a sure money-maker. As we can see on the GMCR charts below, the RSI was trending and the price of the GMCR shares was above the 50 day moving average so it was exhibiting a sort of resistance here.

The MACD below appears to be that of a shorted stock, and in fact at that point in time there was so much of negative news in the market about the company. But like I always said in this kind of situation a seemingly good news could bode well for the shares. And it did!

You see in trading you do not have to be right to make money in the market you just need to do the most reasonable thing. I discussed this in my forex book as well *(Know Why the SOBs on Wall Street Succeed in Trading Forex)*. One golden rule of trading, is that never get in the way of a stock that is exhibiting momentum. Especially one like this.

Any way we entered our trades by purchasing call options. Another factor here is a combination of principle number 2 above. GMCR was shorted, in fact it was well over-shorted in the market at that point in time.

See the marked areas on the chart above. Within 1 week of purchasing the calls on GMCR, I bagged an easy 310% in a week on this single trade. It was a well short-squeezed stock with momentum, and the proven fact...was that it is a momentum stock, and they will move higher despite valuation ratios like P/E and Price to Book that appears totally way out of line. It was a buy because all the analyst predicted a fall and it was well shorted, this is also a short-squeezed stock, omg that day I was dancing all over my office in Indianapolis then. It was the easiest trade I have made in my career.

We constantly make money off this kind of stocks, because value investors would only and always bet against these kind of momentum stocks. Remember, these are momentum stocks. **If they go up by a mere $3.00 on the stock price, a tsunami-happens! Imagine if they go up by about $10.00, this happens, and we have seen over 525% before!** I would show you this with the CMG trade I entered in late November 2013.

Shorting momentum stocks is the most risky thing investors do, **the extreme short squeeze on GMCR in Early 2013 was a blast! 310% in a trade was enough for the month!!!**

Automatic Beta Options Principle #4- the One-touch Effect:

This principle is so obvious that lots of professional traders do not even realize this Guaranteed Profit Signal when they occur and lots of traders have lost thousands of dollars by ignoring them at their own peril. I was stealth on this principle, it was executed with precision on HerbaLife (HLF-NYSE). On August 30th 2013, we purchased HLF Nov 13: 60 Calls for $2.80 and resold them on September 13, 2013 for

$9.20, **228%** return. If you get this 3 times a months are you not going to be pretty good!!!

As soon as we saw our signal we knew the price was going north, and 'there she goes' lovely!!

Just look at the charts below for the stock price and the option price respectively.....

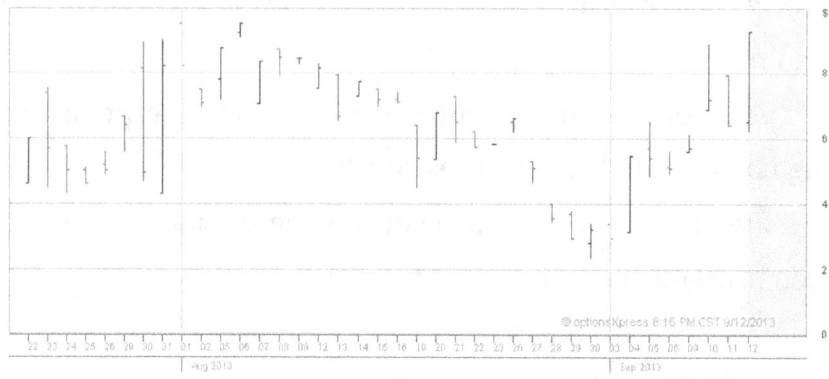

Early September the price of the stock touched the 50 day moving average and it immediately returned to base formation, that is, where it was supposed to be with the rest of the price movement (reversion to the mean). This shows that the market was shaking out weak hands and the stock was ready to continue its ascent. So we bought the options for a pricey sum, yes, but looking backing though we nailed it, it was a sure-fire thing! The rest was history my friends.

I would go through a series of more charts to illustrate the ideas and thinking behind our consistent money making strategies at HiQ Traders Markets Research *(hiqtraders.com)*. This is our art of picking winners, and we do this consistently.

Above you have the chart of BHI (Baker Hughes, In. NYSE) on 17th October, we were following this stock. Then on the 18th of October 2013 chart –see what happened. If you are a subscriber to stockcharts.com you would know that we must have been following this stock to be able to get the chart the day before its bounce. We could not have manipulated the charts. Ok.

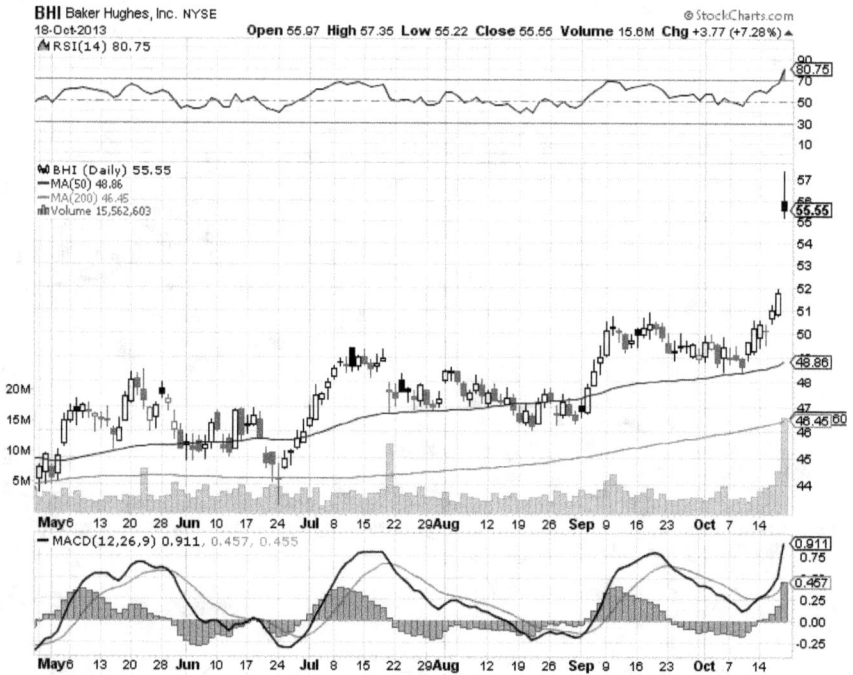

Then next we have the option chart for the BHI Nov 13: 52.5 call. See the move from $1.2 a contract to $4.2 within 24 hours. Yeah, that's what I am talking about.

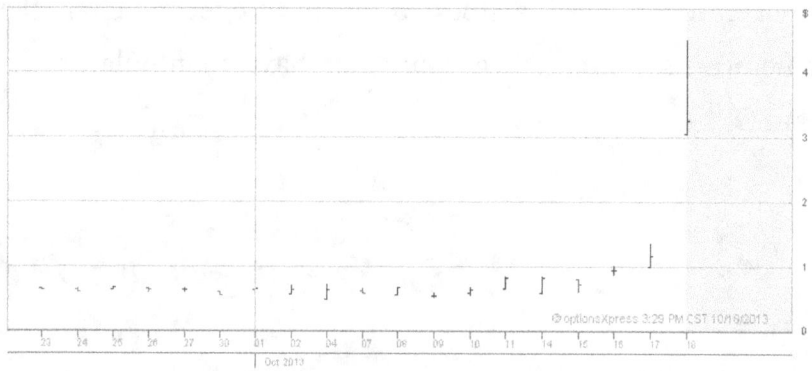

© OptionsXpress.com 2013. BHI Nov 13: 52.5 call

The next chart is for the IRBT, this stock become my candidate when I saw the lines on the MACD come close together and the RSI bouncing back immediately after dropping below the 50 point. So we knew this was another squeezed stock, we capitalised on the drop to enter the trade knowing it had a good support to recover, and it did. We entered the Nov 35 calls for $0.8 and sold within 24hrs for $2.5 per contract.

On that trade our subscribers made a profit of 212.5%, see the option chart below (IRBT Nov13:35call). This is was an effortless trade. You see you do not need to know anything about the stocks once you see the pattern forming, you just need to pull the trigger!

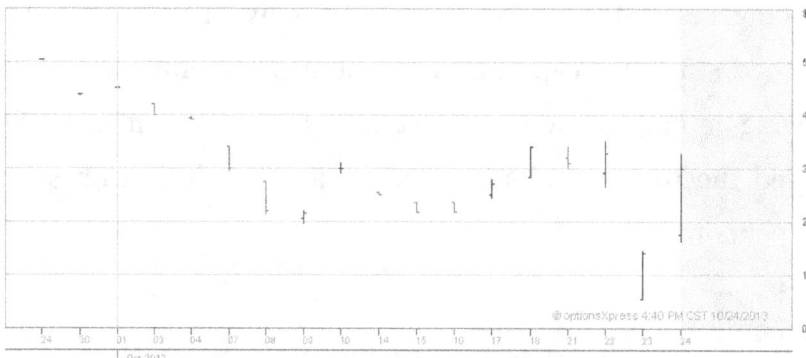

Now look at another wonder trade, it is on Chipotle Mexican Grill (CMG), you could see from the chart below that the MACD is trending up and the stock price as well seems to be well above the 50 day moving average and the RSI keeps retracing above the 50 point mark. Unfortunately the option price was pretty steep.

MAKE MONEY CONSISTENTLY TRADING OPTIONS

So since I knew there was an earning expected, and looking at the options chains, one of the cheapest OTM call was the October 490 calls for $0.85 and resold the nest day for $7.5, a whopping 782.35% gain!

See the options chart below, this is the beauty of buying OTM calls on shorted stocks.

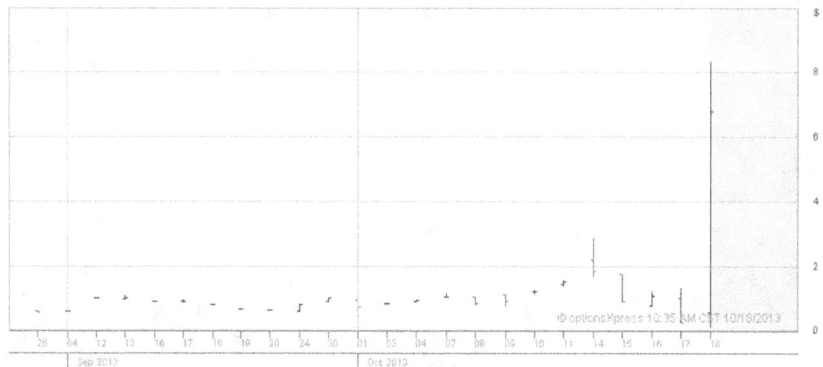

On the day we entered into the CMG trade we entered a GOOG trade as well. Just like CMG it was an expensive stock as well. We bought a relatively cheap OTM Nov 870 calls for $50 per contract and sold it for $ 120 in less than 24 hours, for a 140% gain.

MAKE MONEY CONSISTENTLY TRADING OPTIONS

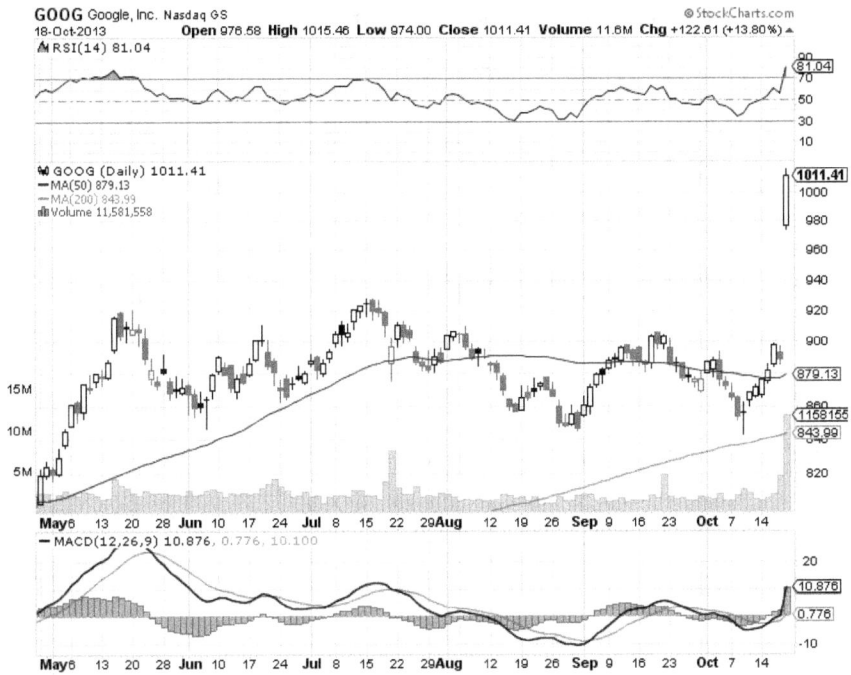

See the options charts below.

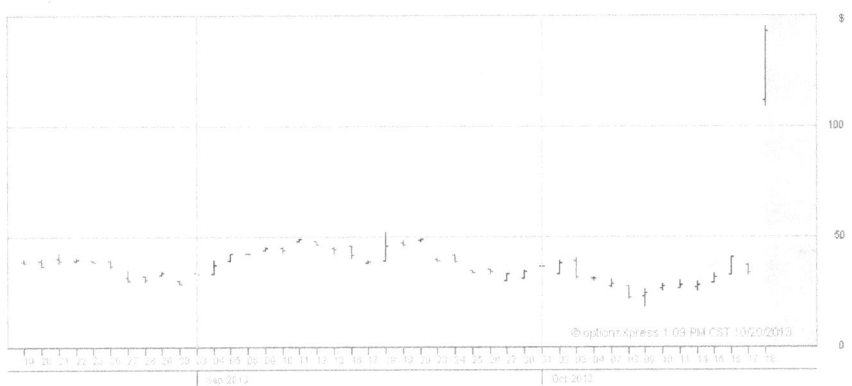

Now let me show one of the few ways we spot put options as well with our visual chart pattern assessments. The stock we would use to explain is our trade on Rayonier (RYN). On the chart by visual inspection you would see that this stock has hit peak of $59 late August 2013, this peak was retested again in late October 2013. Remember the pattern we saw for JOY in the earlier part of this chapter. JOY hit the resistance 3 times and bounced back. When you see this happening it tells you a lot about the market sentiment for this stock. So when I saw this happening I looked straight away at the option prices for this particular stock.

The put options on the stock appeared to be cheap and has been trending on the same price for long time, this is the characteristic behavioural price pattern of the 'long'-squeeze option on a stock. A stock behaviour is seen in the options price pattern and behaviour and ultimately this is the behaviour of the humans behind the prices. And trust me human behaviour never changes.

For the options we decided to buy a very cheap OTM puts, we bought the Nov 2013 55 puts for $0.65 per contract and since we got into this very early with about 4 weeks before the expiration we decided to wait for it to pan out. Lo and behold, the put options jumped to $6.5. We sold out at $5.30, looking back that was premature, as our team could have got an extra profit from a later move during the day, I was in disbelieve! Another 715% gain!

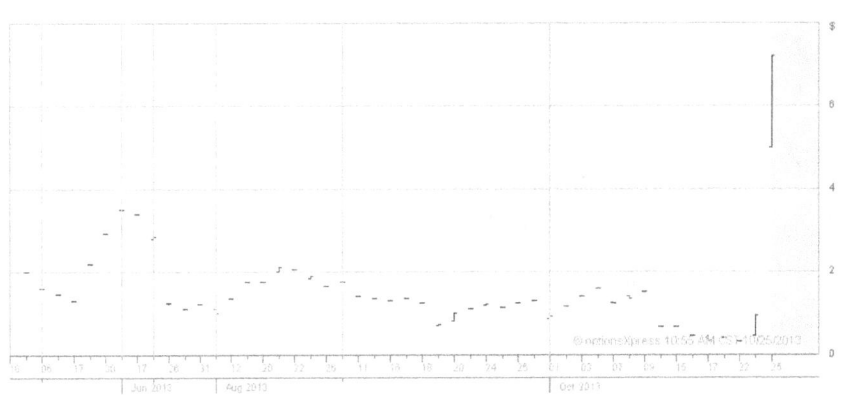

© OptionsXpress.com 2013. RYN Nov 2013 55 puts

More on the entering and exiting puts options; let us look at the Resmed (RMD). It appears to be trending higher over the last few months, but one thing obvious about this stock is its inherent price weakness.

The RSI indicator at the top has been breached twice without significant price extension, the MACD appears to be topping out, and the OTM put options were cheap and they have been cheaply priced for a while. I figured out that it would be cheaper to enter a put on this one and allow it to expire worthless if necessary. The Nov 55 put options were ideal, they were priced at $2.8. So I bought only a few contracts, they were sold for $5 the next day.

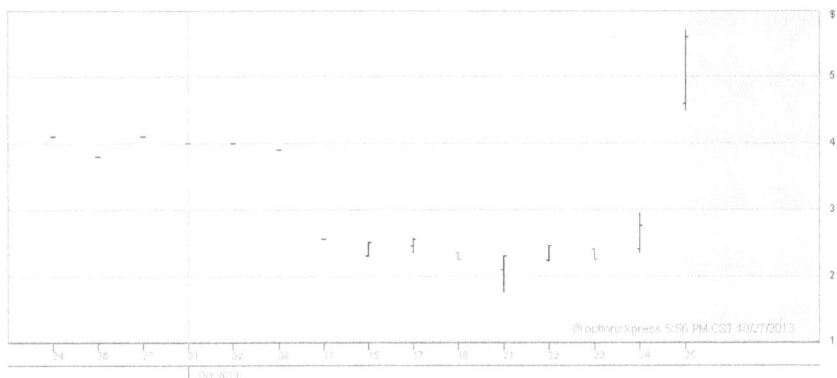

Next, look at the NCR Corp chart below;

On the NCR chart below we could see that the price of the NCR has peaked slightly above $41, and the lowest price was above the 50 MA line. Looking at the MACD below the red and black lines (to simply put them) were very close together, once you see all these 3 signs look at the option chart for confirmation.

When you that see the prices of the options you selected (usually the third away from the at-the-money-price) have been trending on the same price for days, whether as a call or put, in this case put, then you are ready for a kill. I have tested this time and time again. The price pattern on the option contract is the CONFIRMATION.

For example, looking at the put option price chart below, we would see that the price of the NCR November 2013 40 Puts have been trending on the around $1.0 to $1.5 for about 7 days. This is the confirmation I am talking about.

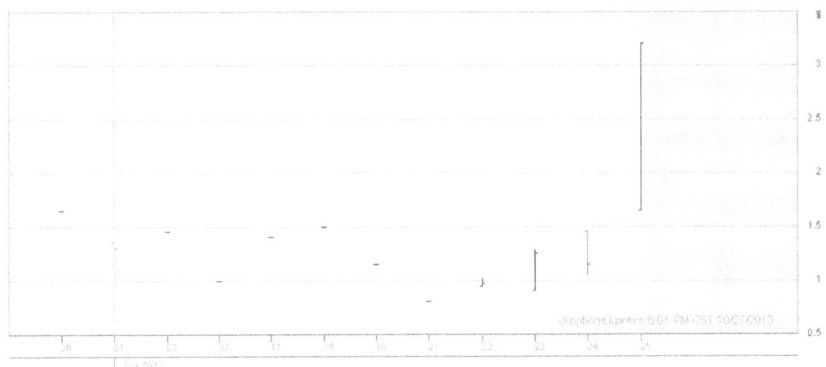

I instructed my team to issue an alert on the put at $1.2 and we sold in 3 days for $2.75, a $129.16% profit, not bad for 10 minutes analysis.

Let us look at the Eastman Chemical Co. (EMN- NYSE). Similar to the chart pattern seen for NCR, we could see that the RSI was having problems surpassing the 70 point mark, this is a warning bell. From the price chart the recent high was around $83 and the recent low was $76. Therefore, we figured out that since it hit that top before and reversed back to them mean (that is, fell), our team position was to short the stock.

The net thing was to look at the put that was OTM and cheap. You see we do not like to spend more than $1,500 on most of our option trades, this gives us the advantage of buying cheap options and making outstanding profits when they move in line with our expectations.

Therefore, we bought the EMN Nov 13: 80 Put at $1.5 and resold for $3.5 in about 48 hours. That was another 133.33% gain. See the stock chart and option call chart below.

We bought the put options at a very low modest price and made a gain of about 133% in less than 2 days.

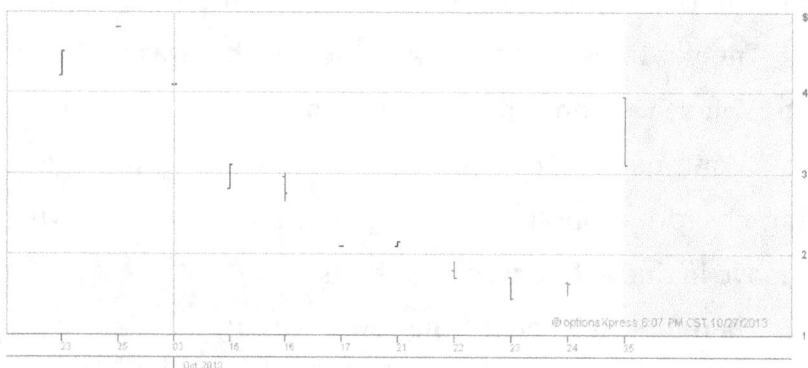

© OptionsXpress.com EMN Nov 13: 80 Put

On the chart below we can see another set up for the Synaptics, Inc. (SYNA-Nasdaq GS), the stock price has hit the peak at $56. On the RSI chart is went above the 70 point mark and appeared overbought. Remember a lot of stocks could remain overbought for a longer than rationally possible (and the opposite is the same). So our analysis was that if the price could be far away from the 50 day MA and it has to reverse to the mean at some point, then a short opportunity might be looming here, at least temporarily.

The put option charts of the November 55 put option appears to be cheapest in terms of the perceived risk here at that point in time when we figured out this trade. So it was purchase at a premium, however to keep in line with our percentage risk capital we bought very few contracts.

The SYNA Nov 55 Put was bought for $4 and resold for $9 for a profit of over 100%.

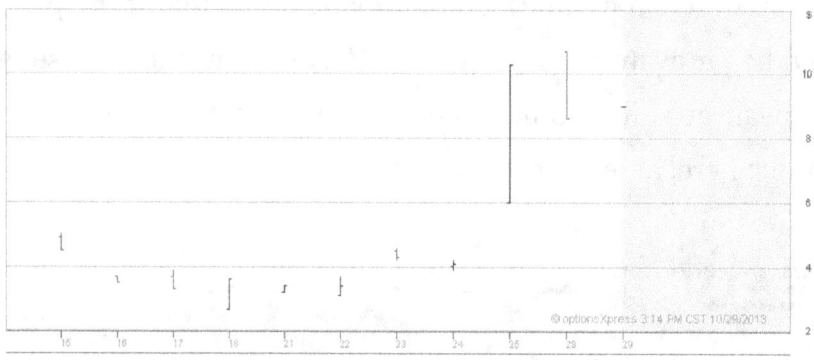

Now to show you the reliability of these visual patterns, look at the Express Scripts, Inc. (ESRX-Nasdaq). Like the SYNA and the EMN charts above, the stock here also has peaked temporarily at $67.5 and made another lower high at $66.5. The RSI has been repelled off the 70 mark, another recent lower high of $65.5 was reached in late October 2013. We decided to look at the OTM put with a cheap option price for maximum gains.

MAKE MONEY CONSISTENTLY TRADING OPTIONS

The ESRX November 2013: 62.5 Put was an obvious choice for us, priced at $1.3 at that time. In less than 48 hours it was ripe for the picking as the put price zoomed to $3.2, we sold out at 2.75. Another gain of 111.5%.

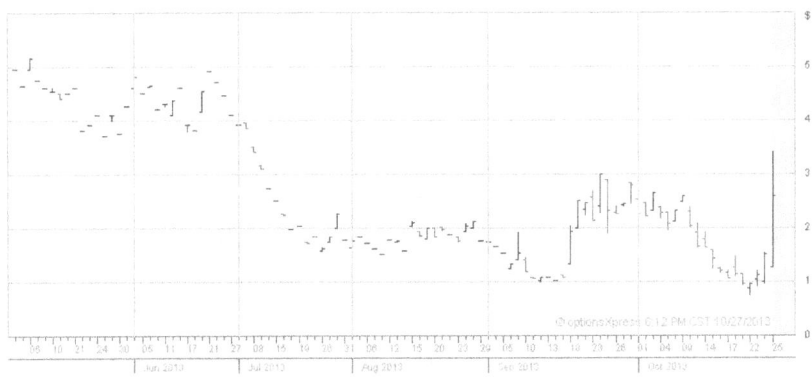

Next see the perfect catch for a call. We caught them unaware on this one, the prices we skewed and the shorts were not covered in time, it was another pounce and bounce trade. This kind of trade could go either way, as it appears to be ready for a pull back.

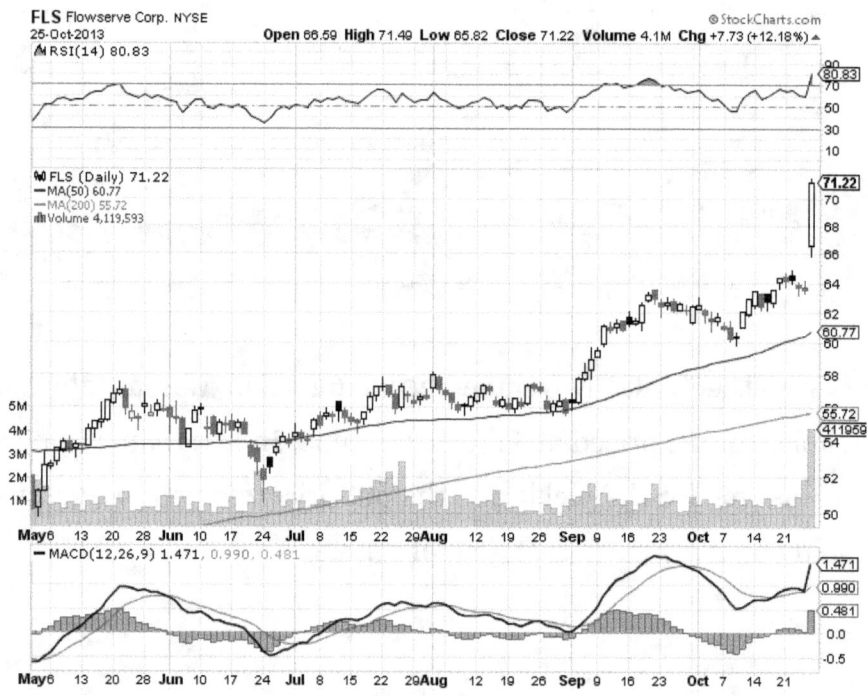

Whenever I see this price pattern on the options charts, I look at the price of the put contract which are few dollars away from the strike price of our chosen option and also the price of the calls. So for the FLS November 2013 65 Call, we look at the FLS November 2013 65 Put; or say the 60put or the

70 put). If the put price also has similar pattern on its price chart, then it is a trade for a spread or strangle, probably not a naked put trade. I would talk about charting and making money on spreads and strangles in my other book. Sometimes for options chart that are obvious you can still make a spread or strangle play on them, but sincerely speaking for what stress.

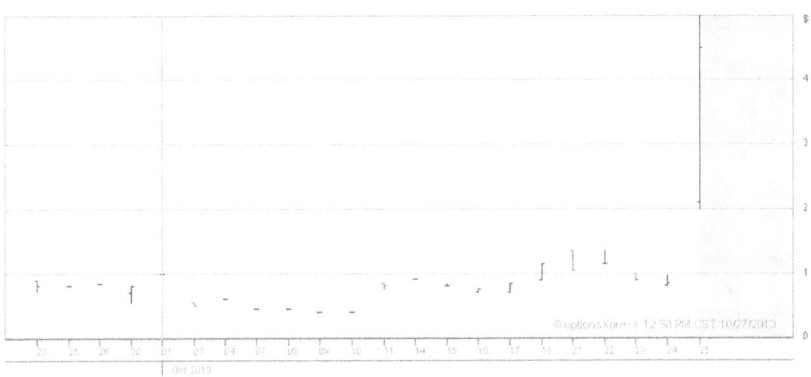

For this FLS we took our bet on the Calls, precisely the FLS November 2013: 65 Call, because the RSI revealed a slight bounce off the 50 point mark. The chart above vindicated us, we bought the options for $1 and sold in 48 hours for $4.2. A profit of 320% by simply looking at the obvious.

The Bristol Myers Squibb Co. (BMY-NYSE) was another case of a short-squeezed stock at it price peak.

The RSI kept above the 50 point mark and the option call were trending and cheap, our losses was considered minimal, and the MACD has been close together for long, a tell-tale of a short-squeeze.

The option chart below shows that the option prices (for the BMY November 2013: 50 Calls) have been ranging between $0.5 and $1.0 for almost a month, this was a recipe for a blast. For your information if you look at the option prices for other ITM or OTM calls you would see a similar ranging price pattern as well.

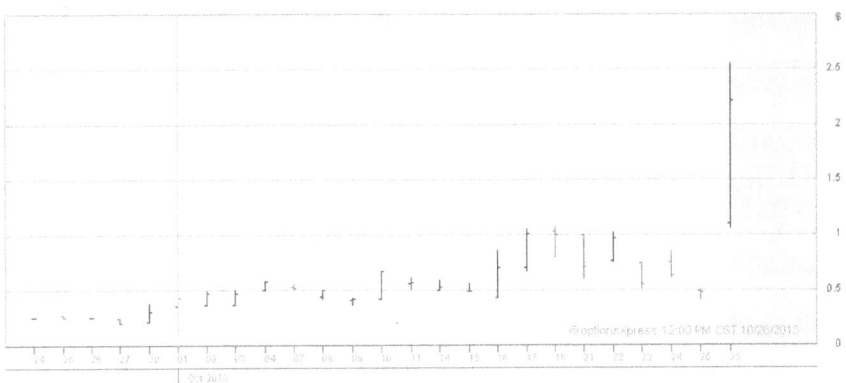

We issued an alert to buy the BMY November 2013: 50 Calls at $0.75 and resold in 2 days for $2.35, making a 213.33% gain.

Let's take a look at Walter Energy a high flyer months and years gone by, which has been trading at a peak of $140 dollar in 2011 and then $80 in 2012. A recent merger acquisition sparked a rumour, and we love rumours and stock splits they are fuels for profit sparks.

See the chart below, the price has been ranging between $14 and $16 and the RSI has been closely trending for a while, coupled with confirmation that the RSI has been bouncing off the 50 point mark. The option chart also revealed a price squeeze pattern like one seen in Facebook and GMCR about mid-2013.

We decided to buy in to this at $0.88, we bought lots of contracts since it was cheap, lol. The next two charts below shows you the fact here, we were paid off in 2 weeks, though a long waiting time, but we made a handsome profit from the trade.

See the next chart after about 2 weeks. The price went up from $15.11 to $19.17 and we sold our contracts for $2.75 each. We made approximately 200% gain on that easy trade. Look at the charts closely, these are secrets you would never find anywhere on this earth.

MAKE MONEY CONSISTENTLY TRADING OPTIONS

See the option chart below for the WLT November 2013: 16 call, it was a whooper!

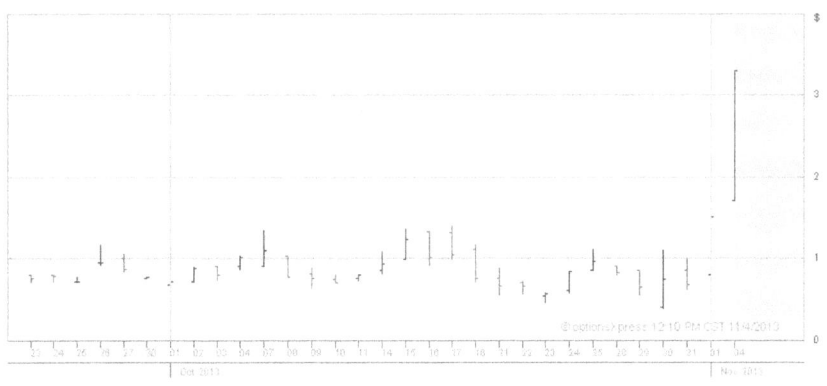

The chart below for Apollo Group, Inc. (APOL-Nasdaq-GS) revealed that for much of October 2013 the stock has been trading around the $20 to $21 price, the RSI looks to be bouncing off the 50 point easily and the MACD appears squeezed, we pulled the trigger when we looked at the option price charts for the stock. It has been trading between $1 and $1.5 over the last one month, it was cheap enough to risk few thousands of dollars. So we bought the calls for $1 and returned in 1 weeks to sell it at $4.5, making a profit of $3.5 on each contract.

Imagine that you bought 30 contracts for $3,000 (30 contracts x 100 share x $1) = $3,000; 100 is the multiplier for stock options contracts.

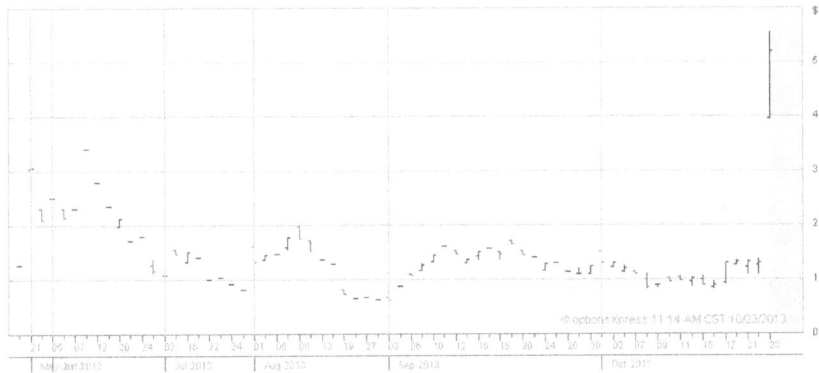

By reselling at $4.5, nets a profit of 350%. This can easily be done, the only thing is to search and know about this stocks before they move, and this is what we do at hiqtraders.com for you.

For CE above, as soon as the price dipped and bounced back above the 50 point mark on the RSI on Oct 6th 2013, and the MACD lines were too close, we were ready for action, the play ensued with a magnificent bounce on the October 21st and an outstanding gain was made. These plays happen every day on the NYSE, NASDAQ, PHLX, and the CBOE daily.

MAKE MONEY CONSISTENTLY TRADING OPTIONS

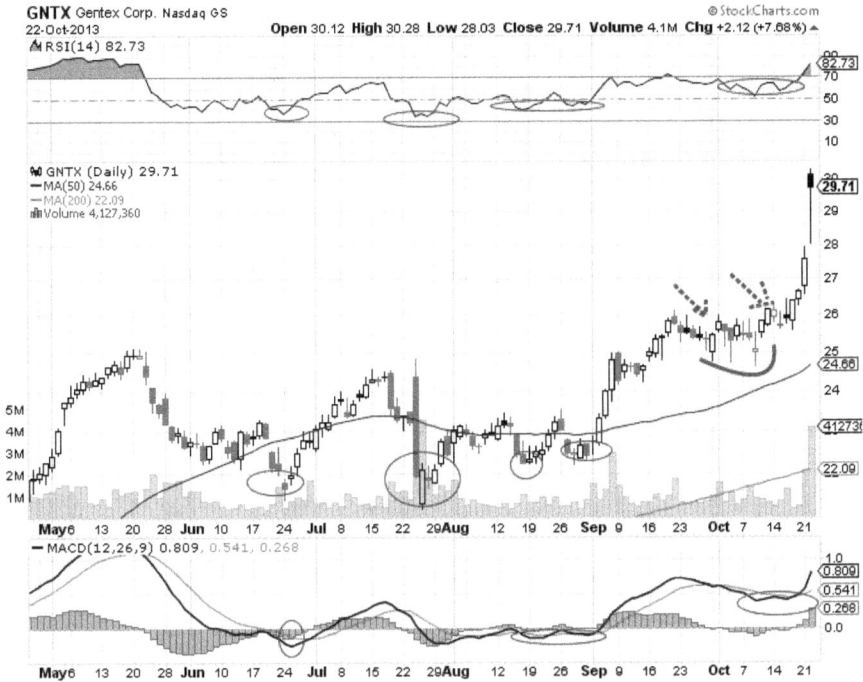

The Gentex Corp. (GNTX – NASDAQ GS) was also a darling, when we saw the signals develop around late September to early October 2013. Looking back this was an easy one, you can see all the marks I made of the charts. There were four bottoms, and each and every time the stock bounced back and recoils. See on the MACD below and the blue curved line on the price chart, the squashing of the MACD line usually indicates a short-squeeze, and this was confirmed on the RSI the price keeps bouncing off the 50 point mark. The option was a ready meat, tasty, nice gains.

You could see similar patterns on the indicators for the CE, GNTX and APOL before the shares sky-rocketed in price.

You don't have to be a genius or an expert analyst to make money, this book puts you in the driving seat, and circumvents the learning curve for you, whether you are a professional or a novice. I am giving you information that is worth more than money you paid for this book, and it is yours for ever. By giving you this book for the token you paid for it it would only be worth something if you made money by using the nuggets shown here. When you do please send me testimonials on support@hiqtraders.com.

The Nu Skin Enterprises, Inc. (NUS-NYSE) was a heavy-hitter, we bought the NUS October 2013: 115 Calls for $2 and resold in 4 days for $7.85, netting a profit of $5.85 on each of the contracts. Our trigger came when we saw the MACD lines close together and the price chart touched the $90 mark and retraced back to where it 'belonged' and the RSI also revealed that the stock rebounded back north on three occasions when it approached the 50 day MA.

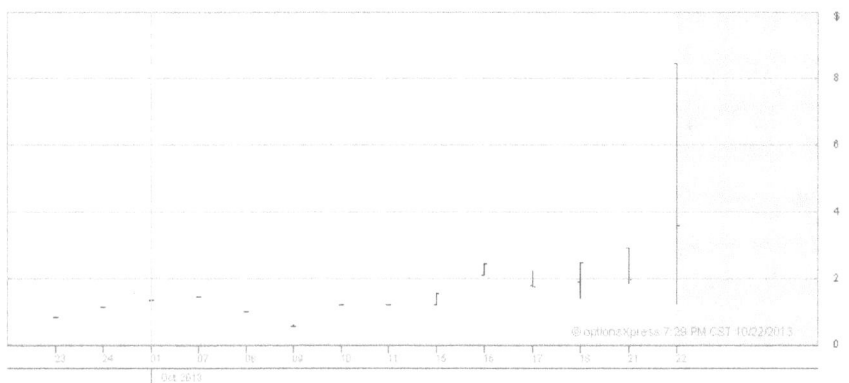

See the NUS October 2013: 115 Calls charts above.

Next, I want to show something fantastic that you hope to happen in your options trading career. See the Cree, Inc. (CREE-Nasdaq GS), the RSI has 'topped' consistently hitting the 70 point mark and retreating, the MACD was clearly exhausted for far too long and ready for a reversal. The stock was trading at $75 apiece.

We played puts on this one, and it was a massive reward for us, this shows how you can make money whether the markets go up or down or whether the stock is up or down. See the next chart below.

MAKE MONEY CONSISTENTLY TRADING OPTIONS

Now the juice came again within one month, this stock Cree, Inc., has rebounded from its low of $54. We saw the RSI *hitting the 30 point mark and not dipping below it*, so we thought it was time to get into calls for this one.

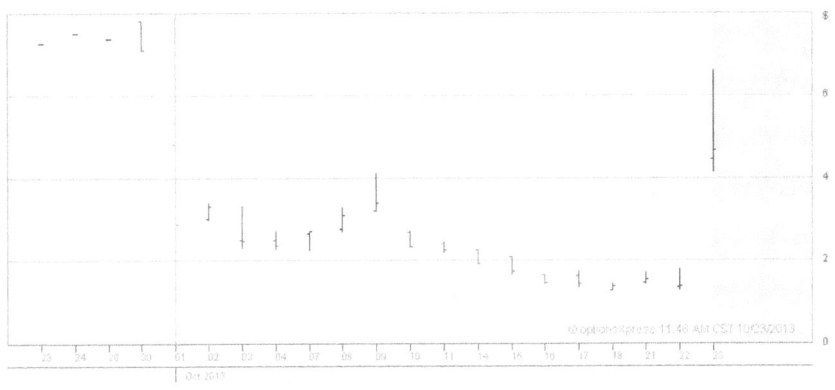

So we bought some calls on it for about $1.5 and resold at $5.75 within 10 days! We entered this stock twice, one on puts and the other on calls, this is how you make money from market gaps in the price of a stock. It must fulfil all the criteria discussed in the chapters before you take such trades.

I would also show you how to milk stocks daily by trading their options back and forth. The obvious examples are th HTZ and JOY.

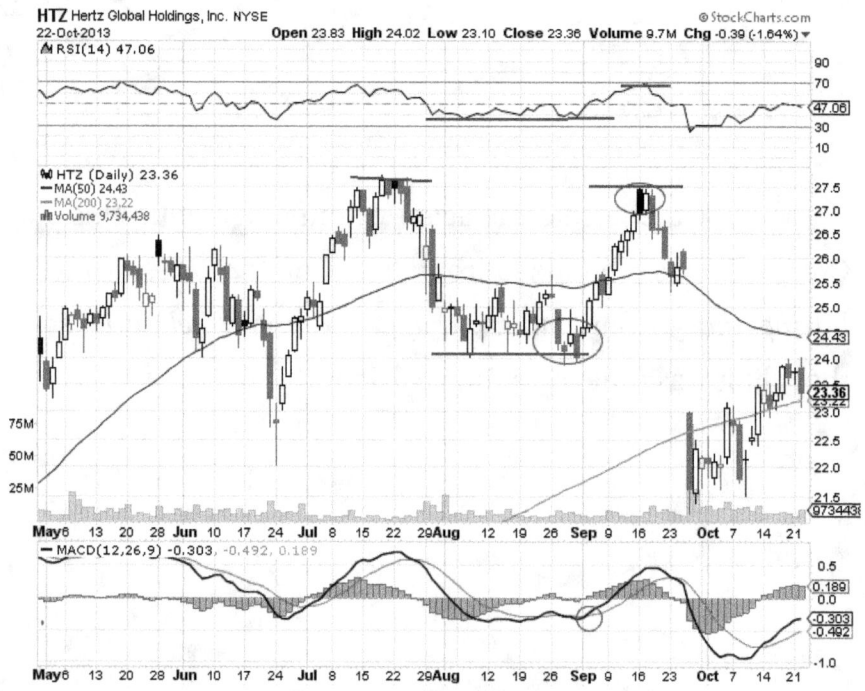

HTZ peaked on or around July 15 2013 at $27.5 and retraced back to bottom at $24 from August 29 to September 9

2013. By September 16, it was back to the $27.5 mark again, and thereafter it fell to a new low of $21.5 by early/mid-October, all happened within three months.

Now you can profit from this up and down moves. Look at the RSI, you would see two markings and lines, these are points where you could buy calls and buy puts respectively on the stock and profit from the upwards and downward moves on the price of the stock.

Now look at the chart of JOY next, like the CREE charts, it swings up and down. Between July 8 and August 27th the price of the stock hit the bottom four times, this is a valid resistance here. I simply bought calls back and forth on this one and I won-all the four.

See the option price charts below.

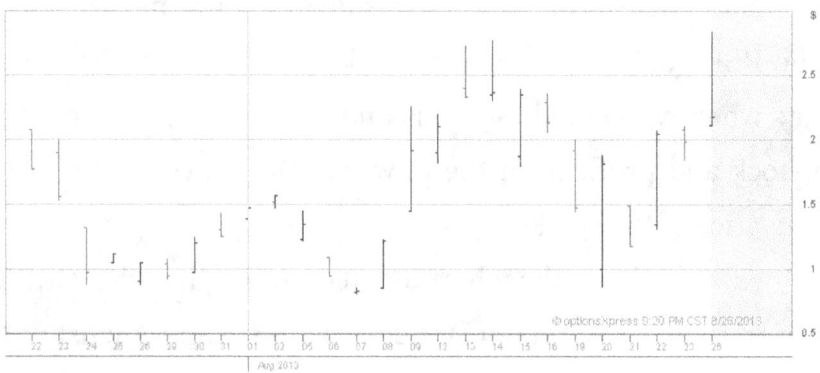

This analysis even works for AAPL, as soon as there was squeeze together on the MACD lines, and the RSI was bouncing off the 30 point bottom mark, and confirmation came from the crossover of the 50 day MA over the 200 day MA, rising almost $30 a share in value over 10 trading days!

All these methods and pattern described above are applicable to the most liquid ETFs as listed in previous chapters of this book. Look at the chart of one of the popular ETF: USO (United States Oil Fund).

And I have compared the price movement of the USO Dec 2013 34.5 Call option on the chart below.

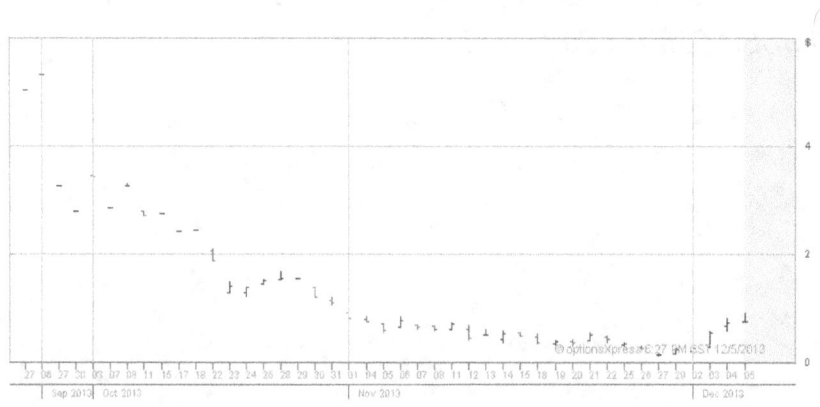

©OptionsXpress.com 2013. Price Chart of USO Dec 2013 34.5 Call on December 5, 2013.

I have also provided a snapshot of the price of this USO Dec 2013 34.5 Call below. Most importantly, to show how thin the spread is: 0.74 – 0.76. If you bought the option contract at $0.08 and resold on Dec 5, 2013 you would have made more than 900% gain.

©OptionsXpress.com 2013. *Price of* USO Dec 2013 34.5 Call on December 5, 2013.

Short interest & Short-squeeze

The secrets that I have shared all rely on *short-squeeze & short interest,* just as liquidity is to the forex market, these two are important in making outstanding returns trading options. Short interest is the number of shares that investors have sold short but that they have not yet repurchased or closed out. It is where the market gets skewed and provides us with opportunities.

Short interest involves borrowing a certain number of shares from the broker with margin (you might be are wondering why would someone do that, well for so many reasons which we have discussed in previous chapters of this book) and then turn around to sell them on the market (that is short sell them) with the hope of repurchasing them at a later date for cheap.

Another important thing, is the short interest ratio (SIR), this is the number of days it would take to cover all existing short positions based on the stock's average daily trading volume. For example, if a stock PRLB trades at an average daily volume of 5 million shares a day, and approximately 25 million of the available shares have been sold short. Therefore the SIR is 5.0 (i.e. short interest / average daily volume).

So once you are in a potentially short stock options trade you would need to have an idea when to close out on the trade, for this you could use this formula as a guide; one must keep an eye on the average change in the volume of shares that is traded, as the average daily volume do change daily.

One more thing, the number of shares available for public trading is the float. That is, for example a stock PRLB has about 20 million shares outstanding and 5 million are owned by insiders, hence they are restricted from trading, the total float would be 15 million. That is, 5 million subtracted from 20 million.

Then the short interest/ float ratio is therefore the number of shares sold short as a total percentage of the floated shares, that is, stock PRLB has a float of 15 million shares, and if 1.5 million has been sold short then the SI/float ratio is 1.5/15 x100% = 10%.

A SIR of about 5 -10 is rare, it is a huge short squeeze opportunity. This works a lot for call when the stocks are highly shorted and trending, and for puts when then are exhibiting resistances in a bull market, as I would show with GMCR puts later.

The mistakes you would need to avoid if you want to follow our approach on trading options are:

1. *You would not need to chase prices:*

The floor traders, just like the brokers in forex, see your orders, and they can know when you are chasing a price, they see your hands, so to say. They have the power to mark up prices of stocks, and even options, increase the spread between the bids and ask prices. Thereby making profits. When you trade our way you tend to get the option prices at the pre-set target price and sell at its peak.

From experience, I have found out that options are better priced (i.e. cheaper) at or around 2 weeks prior to expiration so that is the obvious time to buy. If you see a squeeze set up, and you notice the price of the option contract you intend to buy moving up, simply go for the next cheaper strike price on the option chain. You see when the options prices move they all move in tandem, especially those about $2 strike price up or down the in-the-money strike price.

If for example, say you want to buy the QCOR August 100 puts, but you discover that the price gets consistently marked up, then they is either a good interest in this price or a bad, don't fall for it. Instead of paying *more* for the August 100 puts, check out the August 110 or 120 prices first, ok. However, a slight or few extra cents on the price would not hurt your profit margin, I would either pay a bit more to get in a good set-up than loose it because of a few cents on the option price.

2. You would trade less, make and keep more profits in your account

To make a second career or gains in options trading, it is not how many times you trade. I looked my account at a time, I found that I was taking too many trades, I paid over $4,500 to the brokers in commissions in just 3 months. I was making good profits but I was trading too much. Further analysis revealed to me that the best trades made more profit for less commissions. The secret to making profits in options trading is less is always better. You must always do a total review of your trades/trading account every month or every quarter.

3. If your options spike off with the mid-quarter updates on expected earnings, sell if off straight away, staying away and expecting a further spike with the actual earnings report would do your positions more harm. Only what you banked is yours, paper money or paper profits are not real nor do yours till you cash out.

4. Do not put too much analysis in to a trade, most trade would go bad before they enter in to profits, so give time and allow the profits to pan out.

5. Remember you can never be smarter than the market, it is a big casino, when the money comes to your side of the table take it and run, every man for himself.

Conclusion

In this book I have shown you how I and my team consistent make money from trading options -that is high beta stocks. Now you wonder that if the examples of option trades we have shown you have already taken place how do I still make profits in the future trading these over-squeezed stocks.

Now let me warn you, there would always be opportunities, they are amazing ones every day in the markets, and they will never end. We have a list of high beta stocks that we update every week, and some every quarter and we publish our free trade alerts and the high-profit ones through our hiqtraders.com website for a small fee.

Here you can trade options as a full time endeavour like we do, or part time for your early retirement. The stock market is the greatest invention in the world and leverage is its grandson, and this has been harnessed by the power of trading options today.

Come and join us at hiqtraders.com and start trading today, making it a full time or part time endeavour, we would make it a worthwhile adventure. Trust me!

List of Options Exchanges in the United States

American Stock Exchange LLC
86 Trinity Place
New York, NY 10006 USA
1-800-THE-AMEX
(212) 306-1000
www.amex.com

Chicago Board Options Exchange, Incorporated
400 South LaSalle Street
Chicago, IL 60605 USA
1-877-THE-CBOE
(312) 786-5600
www.cboe.com

International Securities Exchange
60 Broad Street
26th Floor
New York, NY 10004 USA
(212) 943-2400
www.iseoptions.com

Pacific Exchange, Inc.
Options Marketing
301 Pine Street
San Francisco, CA 94104 USA
1-800-825-5773
(415) 393-4028
www.pacificex.com

Philadelphia Stock Exchange, Inc.
1900 Market Street
Philadelphia, PA 19103 USA
1-800-THE-PHLX
(215) 496-5404
www.phlx.com

The Options Clearing Corporation
One North Wacker Drive, Suite 500
Chicago, IL 60606 USA
1-800-537-4258
(312) 322-6200
www.optionsclearing.com

The Options Industry Council
1-888-OPTIONS
www.888options.com

List of ETFs creators

Here are a list of good websites that can be used to research ETFs. When doing your research always remember to make sure you not only know what index, sector or asset class it represents but how it have behaved over time.

Merrill Lynch HOLDRs
http://www.merrilledge.com/investment-products/etf

iShares   http://us.ishares.com/product_info/fund/index.htm

SPDRs   https://www.spdrs.com/

ProShares   http://www.proshares.com/

Vanguard   https://investor.vanguard.com/corporate-portal

PowerShares   http://www.invescopowershares.com/

About the Author

Babajide A. Alalade (MBBS, MD, RICR, DFSRH, DRCOG, MPH Indiana, FRSPH), is an Author, 'Interpreneur', Option, Forex and ETFs Trader, Motivational speaker and a Medical Doctor. He has accumulated years of experience in the financial markets by trading his own money in the Stocks, Options, Forex, and Exchange Traded Funds. He has mentored various traders from different backgrounds and walks of life through his markets trading master-classes which he runs from various locations around the world.

He has meticulously trained himself by studying various charts and books on the markets over the last 12 years. He has learned from experts and has discovered the simple patterns that occur in the markets which has worked for him consistently to make extra-ordinary returns from the markets on a daily basis.

He is the Founder and Vice President of **HiQ Traders Markets Research, LLC** based in the United States. HiQ Traders Markets Research, LLC is one of the nation's leading and fastest growing markets trading signals service with numerous subscribers' base from all over the world.

HiQ Traders Markets Research, LLC (hiqtraders.com) provides daily and weekly market updates and sends signals of our currents trades to subscribers to replicate which has produced outstanding returns month-on-month in the financial markets; Stocks, Options, Forex, and the Exchange Traded Funds.

HiQ Traders Markets Research, LLC

HiQ Traders Markets Research, LLC is a dedicated trading signal service. We provide daily profitable trading strategies for trading the Stock Options, Stocks, Exchange Traded Funds (ETFs) and the Forex markets through our daily and weekly newsletters and emails alerts.

We provide news information including daily market outlook on our website and timely investment reports which are backed by data and results. Our enviable position has been achieved through tireless study of the market and enormous experience from trading the markets through the years.

HiQ Traders Markets Research, LLC as one of nation's leading trading signals providers offers you the best and most effective trading strategies that have been proven to generate substantial profits under all market conditions. We encourage you to stick with our approach as we do see some short-term losses in our trades but overall we turn over profits.

Come ride with us today, and do something today to guarantee your financial freedom tomorrow.

Request any info by sending an email to info@hiqtraders.com, ***or visit our website at hiqtraders.com.***

Further Reading

If you'd like to read more on the underpinnings of options trading, I highly recommend the following books:

- Bittman, James B. *Trading Index Options*. New York: McGraw-Hill, 1998.
- Bulkowski, Thomas N. *Encyclopedia of Chart Patterns*. New York: John Wiley & Sons, 2000.
- Natenberg, Sheldon. *Option Volatility and Pricing*. New York: McGraw-Hill, 1994.
- Nison, Steve. *Japanese Candlestick Charting Techniques*. New York: New York Institute of Finance, 1991.
- Nison, Steve. *Beyond Candlesticks*. New York: John Wiley & Sons, 1994.
- Options Institute Education Division of the CBOE. *Options: Essential Concepts & Trading Strategies*. New York: McGraw-Hill, 1999.

Other Books by the Dr. Babajide A. Alalade

- *Know Why the SOBs on Wall Street Succeed Trading Forex*
- *How to Organise Seminars & Webinars*

Disclaimer

Characteristics and Risks of Standardized Options[3]

Every trader who intends to trade stock options should endeavour to read and understand the outlined purposes and risks of option transactions in the Characteristics and Risks of Standardized Options available from the Chicago Board of Options Exchange (CBOE) at http://www.optionsclearing.com/about/publications/character-risks.jsp

Despite the various advantages of trading options, just like any financial instruments they are not suitable for everyone and certainly not for all investors. You should not enter in to any options transactions until you have performed due diligence to read and understood the risk disclosure document of which link I inserted above. You can obtain it from you broker on request, any of the options exchanges in the United States, or the OCC.

You should ensure that you discuss with your accountant or financial advisor or tax advisor(s) about the implications of buying and selling of options in you accounts or pension funds. This discussions should include margin *requirements, transaction and commission costs, and tax implications of buying or selling equity options*

CFTC RULE 4.41

HYPOTHETICAL OR SIMULATED PERFORMANCE RESULTS HAVE CERTAIN LIMITATIONS. UNLIKE AN ACTUAL PERFORMANCE RECORD, SIMULATED RESULTS DO NOT REPRESENT ACTUAL TRADING. ALSO, SINCE THE TRADES HAVE NOT BEEN EXECUTED, THE RESULTS MAY HAVE UNDER-OR-OVER COMPENSATED FOR THE IMPACT, IF ANY, OF CERTAIN MARKET FACTORS, SUCH AS LACK OF LIQUIDITY. SIMULATED TRADING PROGRAMS IN GENERAL ARE ALSO SUBJECT TO THE FACT THAT THEY ARE DESIGNED WITH THE BENEFIT OF HINDSIGHT. NO REPRESENTATION IS BEING MADE THAT ANY ACCOUNT WILL OR IS LIKELY TO ACHIEVE PROFIT OR LOSSES SIMILAR TO THOSE SHOWN.

U.S. Government Required Disclaimer

Commodity Futures Trading Commission Futures and Options trading has large potential rewards, but also large potential risk. You must be aware of the risks and be willing to accept them in order to invest in the futures and options markets. Don't trade with money you can't afford to lose. This is neither a solicitation nor an offer to Buy/Sell futures or options. No representation is being made that any account will or is likely to achieve profits or losses similar to those discussed on this website. The past performance of any trading system or methodology is not necessarily indicative of future results.

The option quotes and pictures used in these book (or any of its digital products) are only written for illustrative purposes only, they should not be construed as a solicitation to trade a specific stocks, ETFs or option contracts. While they may present an actual price quote it is not intended to be so.

Bibliography

1	Bloomberg, 'Market Vectors Gold Miners Etf', *Accessed from* http://www.bloomberg.com/quote/GDX:US on Dec 3 2013 (2013).

2	Bloomberg.News, 'Paulson's Pfr Gold Fund Fell 16% Last Month to Steepen 2013 Loss', *Accessed from* http://www.businessweek.com/news/2013-10-21/paulson-s-pfr-gold-fund-fell-16-percent-last-month-to-steepen-2013-loss October 21, 2013* (2013).

3	CBOE, 'Characteristics and Risks of Standardized Options', *Accessed from* http://www.optionsclearing.com/components/docs/riskstoc.pdf.

4	———, 'Pm-Settled S&P 500 Options — Updates For: (1) Spx Weeklys; (2) Spxpm; and (3) Xsp (Mini-Spx) by Matt Moran', *Accessed from Also the average daily volume in SPX weekly options has grown from 13,765 contracts in September 2010 to 179,437 contracts in September 2013 on Dec 9,2013* (2013).

5	Citigroup, 'Citigroup Announces Reverse Stock Split Intends to Reinstate Common Stock Dividend of $0.01 Per Share', *Accesed from* http://www.citigroup.com/citi/press/2011/110321a.htm (2011).

6   Daily.Mail, 'The Billionaire Trader Who's Retiring at 38: Hedge Fund Trader and Former Enron Whizkid Reveals He's Giving It All up (but He Has Got $3.5bn in the Bank)', *Accessed from Daily Mail @ http://www.dailymail.co.uk/news/article-2138890/John-Arnold-Ex-Enron-billionaire-trader-retires-38.html* (2012).

7   DirexionShares, 'Direxion Small Cap Bull and Bear 3x Shares', *Accessed from http://www.direxionfunds.com/wp-content/uploads/2013/10/TNATZA-Fact-Sheet-Q3-2013.pdf on Dec 4, 2013* (2013).

8   Forbes, 'Hedge Fund Billionaire John Paulson Lost $736m in Second Quarter Gold Bloodbath ', *Accessed from http://www.forbes.com/sites/afontevecchia/2013/08/15/hedge-fund-billionaire-john-paulson-lost-736m-in-second-quarter-gold-bloodbath/ on Oct 21,2013* (2013).

9   InvescoPowerShares, 'Powersharesqqq', *Accessed from http://www.invescopowershares.com/products/overview.aspx?ticker=QQQ on Dec 3 2013* (2013).

10   Investopedia, 'The 4 Advantages of Options by Ron Ianieri', *Accessed from http://www.investopedia.com/articles/optioninvestor/06/options4advantages.asp Dec 9 2013.* (2009).

11   ishares, 'Ishares 20+ Year Treasury Bond Etf', *Accessed from http://us.ishares.com/content/stream.jsp?url=/content/en_us/repository/resource/fact_sheet/tlt.pdf on Dec 3, 2013* (2013).

12   ———, 'Ishares China Large-Cap Etf Fact Sheet (Fxi)', *Accessed from* http://us.ishares.com/content/stream.jsp?url=/content/en_us/repository/resource/fact_sheet/fxi.pdf *on Dec 3, 2013* (2013).

13   ———, 'Ishares Msci Emerging Markets Etf', *Accessed from* http://us.ishares.com/product_info/fund/overview/EEM.htm *on Dec 3,2013* (2013).

14   ———, 'Ishares Silver Trust', *Accessed from* http://us.ishares.com/content/stream.jsp?url=/content/en_us/repository/resource/fact_sheet/slv.pdf *on Dec 3 2013.* (2013).

15   L. Kroll, 'Billionaire John Arnold Steps in with $10m to Keep Head Start Going During Government Shutdown', *Accessed from Forbes @ http://www.forbes.com/sites/andreanavarro/2013/10/08/billionaire-john-arnold-steps-in-with-10m-to-keep-head-start-going-during-government-shutdown/* (2013).

16   'Monthly Seasonality', *Accessed from* http://www.themarketsbarandgrill.co.za/read.php?3,143 (2013).

17   Nasdaq, 'Ipath S&P 500 Vix Short Term Futures Stock Quote & Summary Data', *Accessed from* http://www.nasdaq.com/symbol/vxx *Dec 3 2013* (2013).

18   ———, 'Spdr Trust Series I Stock Quote & Summary Data(Etf)', *Accessed from* http://www.nasdaq.com/symbol/spy *on Nov. 13 2013* (2013).

19   PowerShares, 'Powersharesqqq', *Accessed from* http://www.invescopowershares.com/pdf/P-QQQ-PC-1.pdf *on Dec 3rd 2013* (2013).

20   Reuters, 'Citigroup Stock Falls Below $1 for First Time, by Jonathan Stempel', *Accesed from* http://www.reuters.com/article/2009/03/05/us-citigroup-idUSN0532847720090305 (2009).

21   SPDR, 'Financial Select Sector Spdr® Fund', *Accessed from* https://www.spdrs.com/product/fund.seam?ticker=XLF Dec 3 2013 (2013).

22   ———, 'Spdr® S&P 500® Etf', *Accessed from* https://www.spdrs.com/product/fund.seam?ticker=spy on Oct. 21 2013.

23   StateStreetGlobalAdvisor, 'Energy Select Sector Spdr® Fund', *Accessed from* https://www.spdrs.com/product/fund.seam?ticker=XLE Dec 4,2013 (2013).

24   Stockcharts.com, 'Put/Call Ratio', *Accessed from* http://stockcharts.com/school/doku.php?id=chart_school:technical_indicators:put_call_ratio on Nov 30 2013. (2013).

25   Wallstreetjournal, 'Soros Fund Bets against Yen, Makes $1 Bln - Wsj', *Accessed @* http://www.reuters.com/article/2013/02/14/hedgefund-yen-sorosfund-idUSL1N0BE0YL20130214. *U.S. hedge fund investor George Soros has gained about $1 billion since November betting*

against the yen, the Wall Street Journal reported, citing people with knowledge of the firm's position. (2013).

26   Wikipedia, 'Pareto Principle', *Accesed from http://en.wikipedia.org/wiki/Pareto_principle.*

27   World.Gold.Council, 'Bringing the Gold Market to Investors', *Accessed from http://wuw.spdrgoldshares.com/ on OCt 21 2013.*

28   Yahoo, 'Guide to the 10 Most Popular Leveraged Etfs', *Yahoo Finance. Accessed from http://finance.yahoo.com/news/guide-10-most-popular-leveraged-152750615.html on November 12, 2013* (2012).

29   ———, 'Ishares Msci Brazil Capped (Ewz)', *Accessed from http://uk.finance.yahoo.com/q?s=EWZ Dec 9 2013* (2013).

30   YahooFinance, 'Ipath S&P 500 Vix St Futures Etn (Vxx)', *Accessed from http://uk.finance.yahoo.com/q?s=VXX Dec 3 2013* (2013).

31   ———, 'Vanguard S&P 500 Etf (Voo) -Nysearca ', *Accessed from http://finance.yahoo.com/q?s=VOO on Nov 13 2013* (2013).